OVER THE HILLS
TO
GEORGIAN BAY

The Ottawa, Arnprior and Parry Sound Railway

OVER THE HILLS
— TO —
GEORGIAN BAY
The Ottawa, Arnprior and Parry Sound Railway

A Pictorial History
of the
OTTAWA, ARNPRIOR
and
PARRY SOUND RAILWAY

by
Niall MacKay

Stoddart

A BOSTON MILLS PRESS BOOK

Engine #611 on the swing bridge at Rose Point. Ontario Archives— Thomas Collection

Copyright © 1981 by Niall MacKay

ISBN 1-919783-06-6

02 01 00 99 98   5 6 7 8 9

Reprinted in 1998 by
BOSTON MILLS PRESS
132 Main Street
Erin, Ontario N0B 1T0
Tel 519-833-2407
Fax 519-833-2195
e-mail books@boston-mills.on.ca
www.boston-mills.on.ca

An affiliate of
STODDART PUBLISHING CO. LIMITED
34 Lesmill Road
Toronto, Ontario, Canada
M3B 2T6
Tel 416-445-3333
Fax 416-445-5967
e-mail gdsinc@genpub.com

Distributed in Canada by
General Distribution Services Limited
325 Humber College Boulevard
Toronto, Canada M9W 7C3
Orders 1-800-387-0141 Ontario & Quebec
Orders 1-800-387-0172 NW Ontario & Other Provinces
e-mail customer.service@ccmailgw.genpub.com
EDI Canadian Telebook S1150391

Distributed in the United States by
General Distribution Services Inc.
85 River Rock Drive, Suite 202
Buffalo, New York 14207-2170
Toll-free 1-800-805-1083
Toll-free fax 1-800-481-6207
e-mail gdsinc@genpub.com
www.genpub.com
PUBNET 6307949

Printed in Canada by Ampersand Printing, Guelph, Ontario

CONTENTS

DEDICATION

To my wife Patricia for putting up with me during the six months that I worked on this book, and to the late J.D.M. Phillips who convinced me that I should write it.

Train Time at Rock Lake. Algonquin Park Museum #2249

A canoe trip embarking at Joe Lake station. Algonquin Park Museum #3123

Deep in the woods on the O.A. & P.S. Algonquin Park Museum #74

Algonquin Park Museum #1162

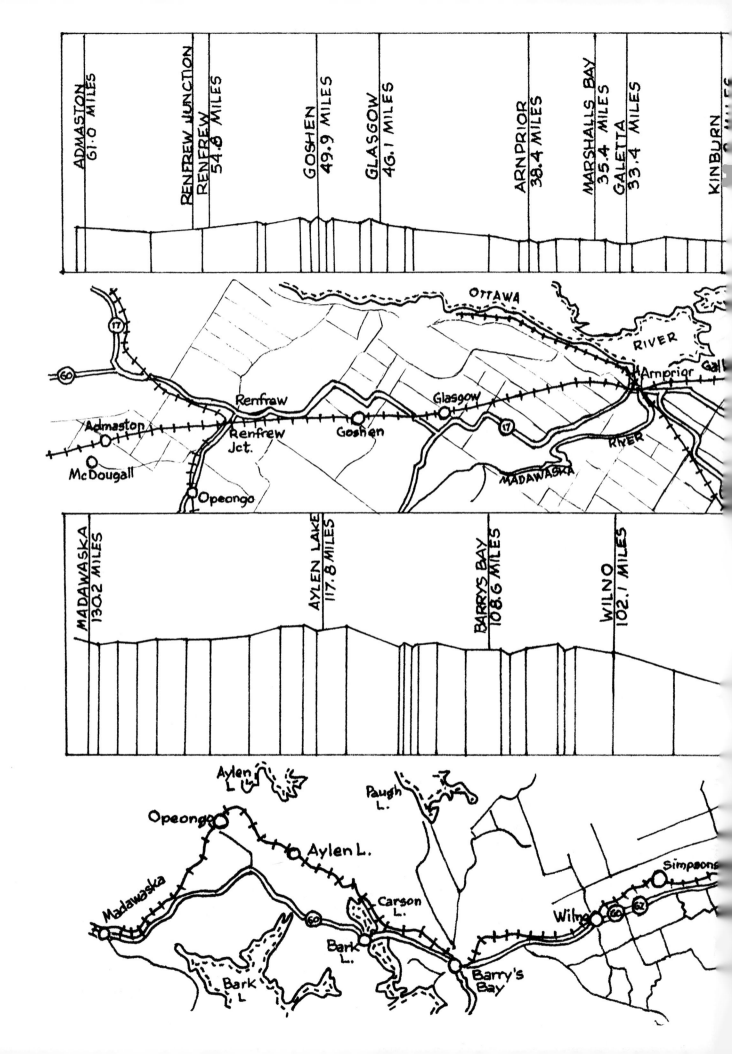

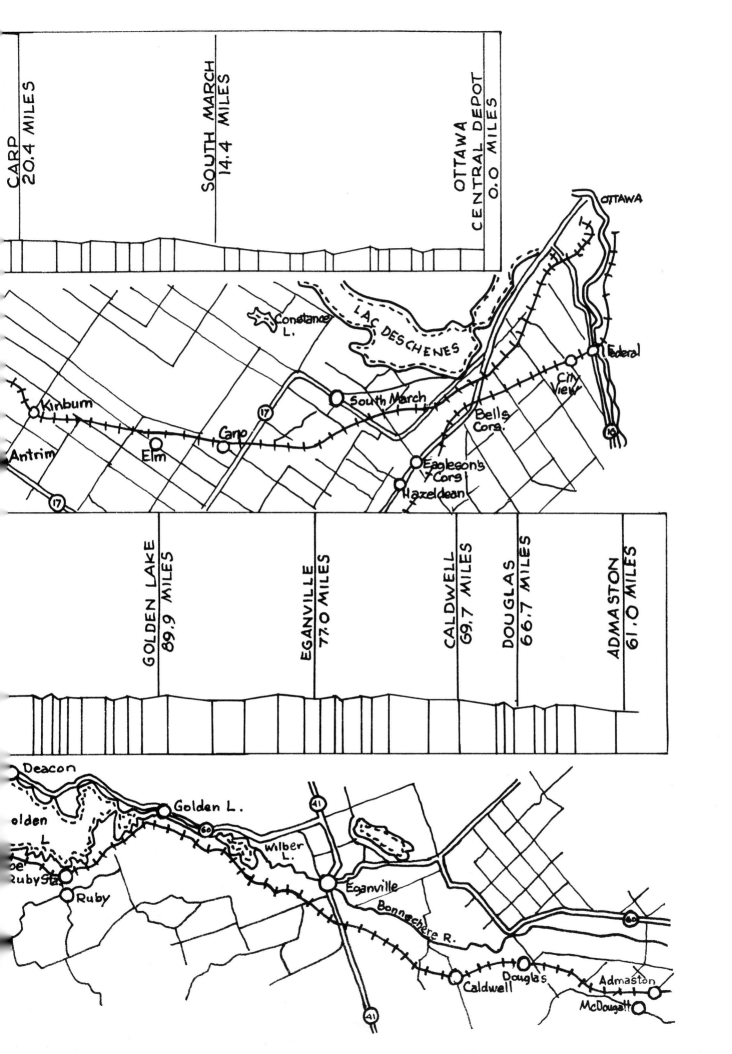

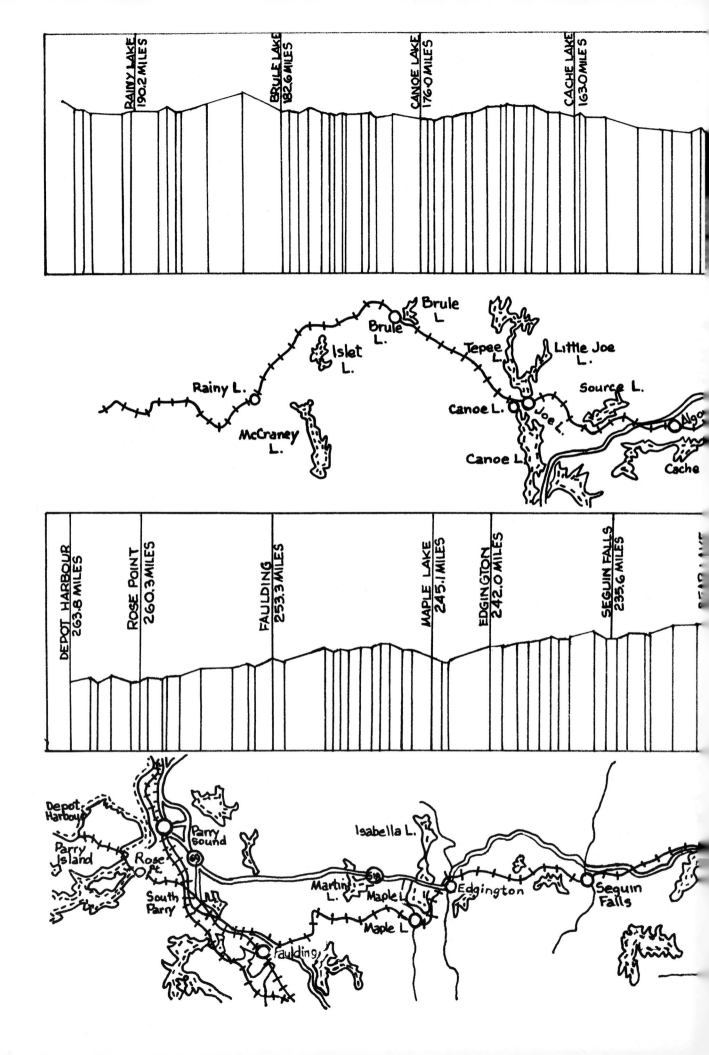

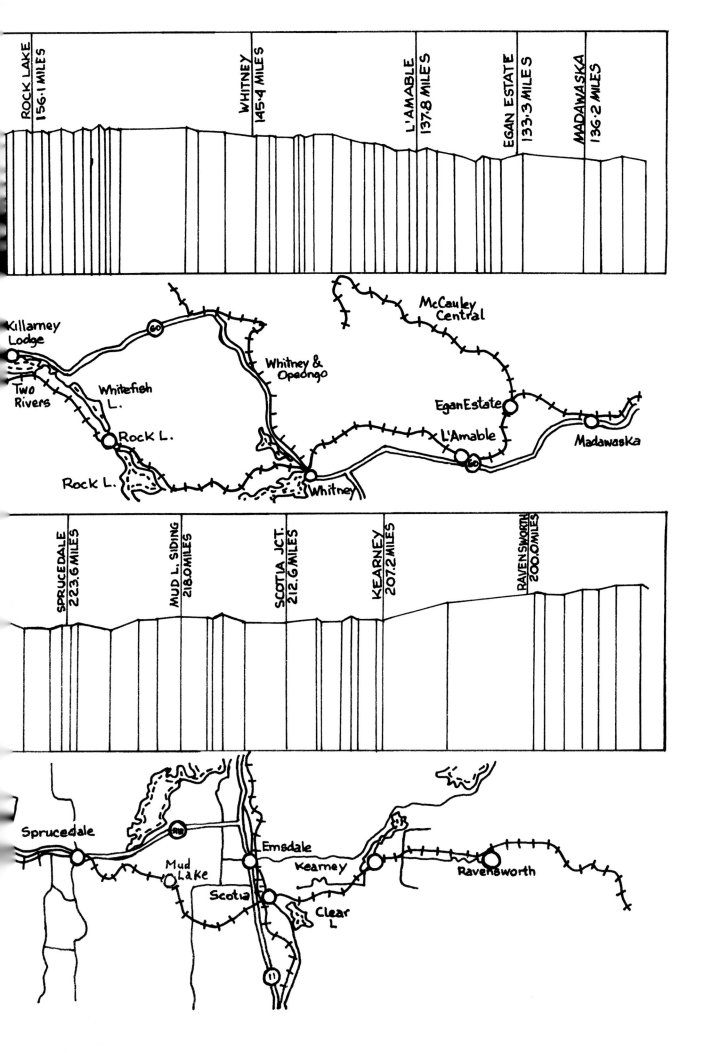

CHAPTER 1
THE MAN BEHIND THE RAILWAY

All railroads have to have a beginning, a source of finance, and a reason for being built. For the Ottawa Arnprior and Parry Sound Railway these three basic factors were supplied primarily by one man, John Rudolphus Booth of Ottawa.

The Ottawa Arnprior and Parry Sound (O.A. & P.S.) came into existence by Act of Incorporation, Chapter 93 54-55 Victoria, assented to 31st July, 1891. This Act amalgamated the Ottawa and Parry Sound Railway and the Ottawa Arnprior and Renfrew Railway, incorporated in 1888.

The reasons for building these railways began in 1879, when lumbermen J.R. Booth and William Perly of Ottawa and G.C. Noble of St. Albans, Vermont, formed the Canada Atlantic Railway Company. This company, made from two earlier railways which had been without financial backing since the depression of 1873, was planned to supply a route from Ottawa to the Central Vermont Railway for export of Canadian lumber to markets in the New England States.

The Canada Atlantic Railway was constructed between 1880 and 1888. Service between Ottawa and the Grand Trunk Railway at Coteau began September 13th, 1882.

By the time that this 135-mile line was completed, J.R. Booth, who was its major stockholder, had incorporated the Ottawa Arnprior and Renfrew and the Ottawa and Parry Sound Railways to act as feeder lines to the Canada Atlantic Railway. He felt that the C.A.R. was not large enough to generate sufficient freight and passenger revenue to become profitable. Two lines had to be incorporated, because the railway from Ottawa to Renfrew was not eligible for subsidy. The Government had already subsidized the Canadian Pacific Railway through the same area. Booth insisted upon building this portion of "the railway to Parry Sound" so that he was not dependent upon the C.P.R. for trans-shipment of freight from Renfrew to Ottawa.

In 1892 J.R. Booth bought control of the Parry Sound Colonization Railway, which, along with the recently incorporated Ottawa Arnprior and Parry Sound Railway, gave him a route from Ottawa to Georgian Bay, an additional 265 miles to feed his 135-mile Canada Atlantic Railway.

Construction began in mid 1892, and by early 1897 service began over the full length of the railway. In 1898, after completing the railway, J.R. Booth organized a steamship company, the Canada Atlantic Transit Company, to transport grain and packaged merchandise from Great Lakes ports in the Midwest to the Maritimes and New England States. His system created the shortest route for goods of this sort, cutting 800 miles off the all-water route through Lakes Erie and Ontario.

In a newspaper interview, Booth considered building the railway further west "to the Pacific if necessary" if the steamship line was not profitable.

In 1899 the O.A. & P.S. was taken over by its parent company, the Canada Atlantic. The Canada Atlantic system was sold in 1905 to the Grand Trunk Railway system for $14 million. This was a loss of $4 million to J.R. Booth.

John Rudolphus Booth, the prime force behind the Canada Atlantic and Ottawa Arnprior and Parry Sound Railways, was also the lumber king of the Ottawa Valley. His sawmills at the Chaudiere Falls had the largest production on the North American continent. The capacity of the mill in 1896 was 120 million feet of lumber a year.

His interesting life started at Waterloo in the Eastern Counties of Quebec on April 5th, 1827. As a child on his father's farm, he was interested in the use of water power and constructed miniature mills on a nearby stream. This interest played a major part in later years, in the harnessing of the Chaudiere Falls in Ottawa to power his sawmills.

At the age of 23, he and his new wife left his father's farm and travelled to Vermont, where he worked for three years as a carpenter for the Central Vermont Railway. In 1853 he returned to Canada and settled in Bytown (present day Ottawa). There he acquired a job in the machine shops and mill of Andrew Leamy of Hull. His resourcefulness and industry were factors which singled him out for promotion, and soon he was manager of the mill. When J.R. Booth was asked to open another mill by his employer, he decided he would strike out on his own.

John Rudolphus Booth of Ottawa, aged 71, one year after the completion of the Ottawa Arnprior and Parry Sound Railway. This man provided the foresight and financing needed to build the O.A. & P.S. Railway as an extension to the Canada Atlantic Railway. This combination created the shortest route between the upper Great Lakes and New England. Public Archives Canada #PA 28000

He rented a mill, only to be burned out a few months later. Turning his back on the ruins, he rented another mill on a one-year lease. At the end of that first year, Booth was so prosperous that his landlord tried to double the rent. Booth refused the increase, and built his own mill on the Chaudiere Falls. One of his first contracts was to supply the lumber for the Parliament Buildings under construction at that time. The profit and bonus from this contract allowed him to expand his mills and timber holdings.

Booth had the foresight to purchase as many timber limits as he could, thereby guaranteeing a source of timber for his mills. In 1867, with the backing of the Bank of North America, he purchased the Egan Estate timber limits for $40,000.00. He was prepared to pay as high as $100,000.00, since his cousin Robert Booth, whom he had sent to inspect these limits, had reported that "the trees were as numerous as blades of grass and of good quality." The high cost of these 150 square miles of timber limits was justified; he was still logging these limits forty years later.

This is an overall view of J.R. Booth's mills in Ottawa around the turn of the century. Public Archives Canada #C5643

Booth was the kind of man who could turn setbacks to his advantage. Three more times, in 1893, 1900 and 1903, Booth's mills were burned down. Each time he rebuilt with better machinery and larger facilities. His mills eventually became among the world's largest, producing, in 1925, 50 to 60 million feet of cut lumber, 4.5 million pieces of lath, 2.5 million shingles as well as paper and cardboard. His timber limits eventually included 7,000 square miles on both sides of the Ottawa River, and he employed approximately 7,000 men in his mills and lumber camps. Booth was an innovative man. It is said that he was the first to use horses instead of oxen for hauling timber. He hired unemployed dock workers, teaching them to use the axe and become lumbermen, because he could pay them less than experienced shantymen. He also was the first in Canada to utilize the eight-hour shift system being used in the United States.

Booth was a good employer. He did not require a man to do a job he would not do himself. At one time he and a crew of men were trying to repair a coffer dam at his Chaudiere mills. When the dam started to give way, they helped him out before climbing out themselves. The dam broke and killed two of these men. In August, 1910, his mills were closed for a week by a strike on the Grand Trunk Railway. Although his workers had done no work that week, he still gave them full pay, as the strike was not their fault. Through acts like this he earned the respect of all his workers.

It is not surprising that this man had so much to do with the building of the O.A. & P.S. Railway. His business capabilities and innovativeness made the Canada Atlantic Railway system the largest privately owned railway in Canada.

This great man was in control of his business empire until shortly before his death on December 8th, 1925, at the age of 98.

This was the man behind the railway.

First and last a lumberman. J.R. Booth, aged 97, shown here beside the last shipment of pine timbers to leave Algonquin Park. These timbers were en route in 1924 to the British Admiralty for decking on their destroyers. Algonquin Park Museum #4133

CHAPTER 2
OVER THE HILLS TO GEORGIAN BAY

The construction of the Ottawa Arnprior and Parry Sound Railway took five and one-half years. During this time the railway experienced many problems, including irate citizens, conflicts with other railways and the roughest topography in Southern Ontario.

Prior to 1891, surveying had commenced on the Ottawa Arnprior and Renfrew and the Ottawa and Parry Sound Railways. After the amalgamation of these two lines, the surveying was completed and construction begun. In 1891 J.R. Booth took over control of the Parry Sound Colonization Railway. In 1896 this line became part of the Ottawa Arnprior and Parry Sound. By keeping the two lines separate, Booth could award contracts for both of them and complete construction over the entire route at an earlier date than would be possible for one railway.

In March of 1893 the first opposition came to light. The Board of Trade of the City of Toronto passed a resolution asking the Provincial and Dominion Governments to stop further subsidies to the O.A. & P.S. Railway. They claimed that their Railway and Transportation Committee "have made exhaustive inquiries as to the nature of the country between these two points, and are assured by Mr. Aubrey White, Assistant Commissioner Crown Lands, and Mr. J.M. Irwin, of Peterboro', who has travelled and prospected this entire region, that, for agricultural purposes, it is entirely worthless, consisting of rock and forest, which will never admit of settlement or cultivation, and which is without any existing population, and without even mineral wealth, as far as at present discovered."

Their Committee was of the opinion "that the Council should take active steps to influence the Government against further assistance to a Line which is being constructed principally in the personal and business interests of its promoter, for a long distance through a country entirely useless for settlement or agricultural purposes, and which when completed will very seriously affect the Commercial interests of Toronto and Western Ontario, by diverting to Ottawa, Montreal, the Canada Atlantic Railway and its allied American Lines, the trade we now enjoy. We submit that the completion of this Line to Parry Sound will not develope or increase the prosperity of the Georgian Bay country, but merely throw to other channels the trade now served from Toronto and Western Ontario.

"Your Committee further submit that the construction of this Line will adversely affect the interests of Lines of Railway already projected, partly constructed and in operation from Toronto, Whitby, Port Hope, Trenton, Belleville, Deseronto, Kingston and Brockville, for which subsidies have already been granted by the Dominion and Provincial Governments and interested municipalities, by diverting from them traffic to Ottawa, Montreal and the East, which they were projected to secure for our City and other Ports located on Lake Ontario, thereby nullifying the results expected from these Branch Lines, for which the taxpayers of Ontario have already been called upon to pay such large amounts."

Similar resolutions were passed by the Municipalities of Trenton and Port Hope. No government action was forthcoming; and the O.A. & P.S. continued to receive the standard subsidy of $3,200.00 per mile and a double subsidy of $6,400.00 per mile for some of the more difficult trackage.

Meanwhile, the O.A. & P.S. had taken another railway to court. The Atlantic and Northwest Railway Company (later part of the C.P.R.) had filed a survey route through Hagarty Pass west of Eganville. This route duplicated that of the O.A. & P.S., which had already been surveyed and graded. The court Declaration of April 21st, 1893, cancelled the survey route of the Atlantic and Northwest Railway Company and refused them the right to cross the O.A. & P.S. This action effectively curtailed any expansion past Eganville by the Atlantic and Northwest.

On September 13th, 1893, the first 35½ miles of the railway, from Ottawa to Arnprior, were opened for public traffic. The O.A. & P.S. now came into conflict with the Canadian Pacific Railway. An overhead crossing of the C.P.R. tracks in Nepean Township had been built with the understanding that they would be allowed a level crossing with the C.P.R. in Arnprior. The C.P.R. disagreed, and wanted another overhead crossing. That would have caused the O.A. & P.S. to construct embankments within the Town of Arnprior at great expense.

The conflict ended with a ruling by the Board of Railway Commissioners which allowed the O.A. & P.S. to construct a level crossing no nearer than 500 feet west of the C.P.R. station. This would allow long trains to be clear of the crossing when stopped at the station.

With the resolution of this conflict, construction continued and a further two sections, from Arnprior to Renfrew and from Renfrew to Eganville, were opened in December 1893.

The railway, to this point, had been constructed through agricultural land; this had necessitated fencing, road and farm crossings, and the occasional bridge, but had provided no major construction problems. Twenty miles west of Eganville the railway began the ascent through Hagarty Pass to the Algonquin Highlands, a continuous climb of 425 feet in nine miles at an average of point nine percent grade.

The Inspection Report for the third ten-mile section west of Eganville, written by Thomas Ridout on October 9, 1894, gives the following information.

"The sharpest curve being 6° — 955 ft. rad. and steepest grade 67 ft. per mile." The right of way was cleared "to the full width of 50 ft. on each side of centre" complete with fencing "consisting of 4 strands of barbed wire and top board on cedar posts set 12 ft. apart."

There were 4 public road crossings and 20 farm crossings. Embankments were 15 feet wide, and cuttings were 20 feet wide with good ditches. Forty-two culverts, and one bridge with a 17-foot clear span, were required.

The track consisted of 72 lb. rail on ties of tamarack, cedar and hemlock laid 2800 to the mile, with 10 inches of ballast throughout.

The estimated cost of this section of railway was $153,466.00. This included a subsidy of $33,600.00.

The railway now entered an area of rolling terrain which would require many embankments. As the closest supply of fill would not be reached until further construction had been completed, the company received permission to construct temporary trestles in the next 37 miles. Sixty-five trestles, totalling 5.91 miles, were built. These structures were up to a third of a mile long, 15 to 30 ft. high, with grades up to 1.2% and with curves as sharp as 6°. They were built from 15 in. diameter pine posts with 14 ft. long 12 in. thick flattened cap timbers and 5 in. thick braces. All the timbers were spiked rather than bolted, as they were intended to be temporary structures only. Trestles over 20 ft. high were built in two levels. By agreement, temporary trestles of this sort had to be converted to embankments by filling within two years of their building date.

A large yard containing about 1½ miles of sidings was constructed at Whitney for the shipment of lumber from the St. Anthony Lumber Company. There was a ¾ mile branch to the mill. This lumber company had been built at Whitney because the railway would be able to service it.

The next 17-mile section was relatively easy to construct, as it roughly followed the shores of Long, Rock and Whitefish Lakes, ending up at Lake of Two Rivers. From Whitney it climbed at an average of 16 ft. per mile for three miles, then continued almost level for the next 14 miles, dropping only 28 ft. in that distance. Because of the difficulty in obtaining fill, 17 temporary trestles were required in this section. Two wooden bridges were constructed over timber roads used to transport logs to the lakes for the spring log drives. Two trestles of over 1,000 ft. each were constructed on foundations of rock-filled cribs to cross two bays where rock bottoms did not allow driving piles.

The remaining 51 miles from Lake of Two Rivers to the crossing of the Northern and Pacific Junction Railway at Scotia would prove to be the most difficult and costly section on the line. To reach Scotia, the railway had to cross the divide separating the Muskoka and Georgian Bay watersheds from the Ottawa Valley watershed. One hundred and one culverts, numerous rock cuttings, 57 temporary trestles, 20 permanent trestles, three steel bridges and one 550-ft. long and 76-ft. high steel trestle were required to build this section.

These 51 miles consumed 144,623 cubic yards of ballast, 142,576 ties and 4,563,786 board feet of timbers which averaged 12 by 12 inches in cross section. The total cost was $1,115,061.93, or an average of $21,808.00 per mile.

The railway reached Scotia in December of 1896, where it joined with its Parry Sound Colonization Railway section.

Construction on the Parry Sound Colonization Railway had begun in 1886, with the laying of track with 50-lb. rail. After completing only ten miles west from Scotia, the company ran out of funds. This railway remained dormant until 1891, when J.R. Booth bought control. Construction was restarted with the replacement of the 50-lb. rail by the standard 72-lb. rail being used on the Ottawa Arnprior and Parry Sound Railway.

The railway from Scotia to Rose Point passed through vast tracts of swamp, sand and rock, with few areas of agricultural land. Construction of many rock cuts, embankments and temporary trestles was required before the line reached Georgian Bay.

Construction was completed on this line by July, 1895. The Parry Sound Colonization was amalgamated with the Ottawa Arnprior and Parry Sound in October, 1896. The first through train over the joint lines ran on January 7th, 1897.

The railway would not be complete, however, until it crossed onto Parry Island from Rose Point, and the remaining 3.45 miles to Depot Harbour had been constructed. This would not occur until later in 1897.

In March of 1897, the Minister of Railways received two documents expressing displeasure with the railway. The electors of the Electoral Riding of South Renfrew signed a petition against the railway. They were upset because the O.A. & P.S. was constructing its division point at Madawaska, "a place which is a complete wilderness wholly uninhabited and of considerable distance from any settled district but in the midst of Mr. J.R. Booth's timber limits."

They felt that Barry's Bay, which was situated "in a level, well-settled country and in the neighbourhood of the populous villages of Combermere and Rockingham", was the natural division point for the railway. It was "an outrage that the Government permit the said railway company to place the divisional point at Madawaska instead of Barry's Bay where land can be purchased for $50.00 per acre and where it would be of immense benefit to the surrounding municipalities and to the country which aided in its construction."

They also wanted the railway to pay $1,500.00 for materials and supplies provided by the settlers along the route, payment being long overdue.

The second document that the Ministry received was a letter from Mr. Frank Stafford, a landowner from Barry's Bay. In 1894 Mr. Stafford offered the O.A. & P.S. the right of way across his property according to their registered survey plan. He also offered two acres free for station grounds. The railway, however, re-surveyed that section of their line, and when constructed it was 90 feet nearer to Mr. Stafford's buildings. They also erected a water tank at his back door.

Mr. Stafford objected, and requested payment for the station acreage on the grounds that it was not the same plot he had originally offered. To compel Mr. Stafford to deed the property to them, the railway closed the station for five months, replacing it with a temporary station two miles down the line. This action resulted in a petition from the local residents to the Ministry of Railways and Canals, trying to rectify the situation. Indirect pressure was also brought on Mr. Stafford to come to some decision with the railway. Frank Stafford reached an agreement with J.R. Booth, allowing use of water from the tower for household purposes and fire protection in exchange for the deed to the station property. However, the provision for water was not written into the deed, as it would not apply to Frank's heirs. A separate agreement was forwarded to Frank Stafford for his signature. This agreement gave him the water he requested, provided sufficient water was available.

By 1897 Frank Stafford had received little water from the tank, as the railway claimed they had only enough for their usage. After many attempts by his solicitor to obtain more water, the railway now refused to allow the use of water under any consideration. Frank Stafford requested that the "Government give no further subsidy to a railway company that obtained land under such circumstances and thereby invest them with further power to coerce one of your followers who has given many years of party service."

The equipment and transportation used in the survey of the Ottawa and Parry Sound Railway near Eganville in 1890. Public Archives Canada #PA 122508

No action was taken on either document, and the division point remained at Madawaska and the railway was paid further subsidies. By June of 1897 the remaining 3.45 miles of railway had been constructed. This portion required a great deal of earth before tracklaying commenced. The sub-contractors, Brewder and McNaughton, report excavating 54,329 cu.yds. of earth, 206 cu.yds. of loose rock and 11,363 cu.yds. of solid rock in this 3½-mile section. The railway itself reported another 89,654 cu.yds. of earth and 770 cu.yds. of solid rock removed from the harbour shore area.

A double track pile trestle 2,300 ft. long was constructed in an average 20-ft. depth of water. Eight piles to the bent, with a 30-ft. cap beam and stringers of 15 by 16 inch pine, were used in its construction. This trestle was constructed beside an extension dock on which two freight transfer warehouses were built, one 80 by 600 ft., the other 80 by 700 ft. The total cost of this portion of the railway, including an engine house, turntable and dock trackage, was $80,444.30.

The railway was now complete. It still received one more petition in mid 1899, this one from the Town of Parry Sound.

The petition requested the construction of a spur line from the Ottawa Arnprior and Parry Sound into the Town of Parry Sound.

The O.A. & P.S. had departed from the original survey route of the Parry Sound Colonization Railway, bypassed the Town of Parry Sound and constructed its own town at Depot Harbour. The reason commonly given for this action was that J.R. Booth considered that the prices of dockspace in Parry Sound, requested by the town, was too high. Although this may have been an important factor, the surveys had shown that Depot Harbour was the best natural harbour in the Great Lakes. This was probably the main reason for building there.

This did not suit the people of Parry Sound, as it meant transporting any produce or merchandise to and from Rose Point by boat. The James Bay Railway was incorporated by Toronto businessmen primarily to build the spur from the O.A. & P.S. into Parry Sound, although its charter authorized a railroad from Toronto to Parry Sound and further north.

At the request of the Government the O.A. & P.S., now part of the Canada Atlantic Railway, constructed and operated the six-mile James Bay Railway. Passenger service between Parry Sound and James Bay Junction consisted of one coach and a Canada Atlantic locomotive once a day. It remained more convenient for passengers to travel to Rose Point by boat to catch trains to Ottawa.

After only a few years of operation, this line was sold to the newly formed Canadian Northern Ontario Railway and ceased to be operated by the Canada Atlantic.

The Ottawa Arnprior and Parry Sound Railway had been difficult to build, but once constructed, it and the Canada Atlantic Railway were the shortest route from the upper Great Lakes to the east. At its heyday in 1910, enough traffic was generated to require one train every twenty minutes over its single track mainline.

Surveying was a year-round job which continued for many years. This crew was photographed near Golden Lake in the winter of 1890. Public Archives Canada #PA 122500

Survey camps had all the comforts of home, including a haircut. Engineers' camp near Ravensworth, winter of 1895. Algonquin Park Museum #129

Earth cuts were excavated at many places using men with shovels. Algonquin Park Museum #156

A horse drawn grader of the type used during the construction of the O.A. & P.S. is shown here on exhibit at the Gravenhurst Centennial display. Algonquin Park Museum #2426

One of the many temporary trestles under construction. Note that the far end has been built in two levels, as it was over 20 ft. high. Algonquin Park Museum #125

Another view of a temporary trestle. Note the rounded cross braces and variety of rock sizes used in the approaching embankment. Algonquin Park Museum #152

Many rivers were crossed along the right of way. The masonry abutments on this bridge over the Madawaska River were typical and can still be seen today. Algonquin Park Museum #168

Rock cuts were blasted and the rubble removed by man and horse, The log rails provide a skidway for the stone boats hauled by the horse. Algonquin Park Museum #123

The temporary Islet Lake trestle. This "S" shaped trestle was later filled in to become an embankment.
Algonquin Park Museum #143 — #132

Where soft lake bottoms permitted, pile trestles were constructed across small bays. Shown here is the floating pile driver used in Rainy Lake, 1896. Algonquin Park Museum #146

A typical construction camp on the Parry Sound Colonization Railway section of the Ottawa Arnprior and Parry Sound Railway. Ontario Archives Acc. 10328, Tray 4 #46

Cashman Creek Bridge under construction in Sept., 1896. This bridge, 550 ft. long and 78 ft. high, trembled when trains crossed it. Note the special crane used to raise sections of the bridge. Algonquin Park Museum #133

CHAPTER 3
OTTAWA TO DEPOT HARBOUR ON THE CANADA ATLANTIC

Let us now travel back in time and take a trip on the trackage of the Ottawa Arnprior and Parry Sound Railway, part of the Canada Atlantic Railway.

The date is June 23, 1905. It is 11:30 in the morning on a beautiful sunny Friday. As we board the equipment of 1st Class Train No. 52, to reach our seat we pass the smoking room with its straight back leather seats and wall mounted mirrors. The main coach section is equipped with horsehair cushioned reversible seats. I marvel at the polished hardwood trim with its delicate inlays and the brass lamps hanging overhead. The Dominion Parliament Buildings can be seen out the window in the background.

Upon leaving the station at 11:55, we pass by numerous small companies whose freight sheds are served by the railway. At the foot of Elgin Street we pass through the Canada Atlantic's freight yards. Within a very short time we have left the city behind and are travelling through farmland mixed with woodlots.

We stop momentarily at a small lineside building which I am informed is the "station" for South March. One of the local women is returning from a visit to her sister in Ottawa. We start on our way and within ten minutes we stop again, this time at Carp. The station here is a beautifully designed two-storey building with an attached freight shed. I will come to recognize this as the standard style of station used on this railway. We continue on our journey with frequent stops, as this part of the country is well populated, with small communities every few miles. At Galetta we pause to take on water before proceeding to Arnprior. We have been travelling at an average of 35 miles per hour, including stops.

Arnprior is the first major town of any size that we have come to. The station, a long single-storey structure, has more waiting room space than any other station we have encountered so far.

We leave Arnprior at 1:00 p.m., cross over the C.P.R. tracks and continue towards Renfrew. At Glasgow, seven and one-half miles west of Arnprior, we come upon Train 61, an eastbound way freight waiting patiently on the siding for us to pass. We are still travelling through farming area, although there are more woodlots than before and fewer homesteads can be seen. We pass a flagstop station called Goshen and finally arrive in Renfrew. Train 60, the westbound way freight which left Ottawa at 7:20 a.m., is switching cars in the yards when we arrive. One mile out of Renfrew we stop to pick up passengers from the Kingston and Pembroke Railway, known locally as the Kick and Push because it runs so slowly, at Renfrew Junction. We are leaving the flat country behind and entering a region of gently rolling landscape, with large areas of forest visible from time to time. Our train pauses for water at Eganville Station before proceeding to Golden Lake. Upon reaching the station, we learn that there will be a ten-minute delay. Train 53, the eastbound passenger train, was delayed while a farmer chased his wayward bull off the tracks. While we wait we exchange passengers with Train 46, which makes the half-hour trip on the Pembroke branch.

At Killaloe we again stop for water, as much steam will be used in the climb towards the Algonquin Highlands region. The railway now begins to wind its way back and forth between little hills and then bigger hills as we climb higher.

The train stops briefly to let off passengers at the community of Wilno, the first Polish settlement in Canada. We continue to wind our way up to a small pass. As we cross the summit the train begins to pick up speed. The next five miles, through forested terrain, pass very quickly and we find ourselves in Barry's Bay on Lake Kaminiskeg. As the engine tops up with water, I look across the tracks at the Opeongo Hotel, which was built in 1882 to service travellers on the Opeongo Colonization Road.

We depart at 3:20 p.m. and begin to climb again, following the shore of Carson Lake before crossing over Hagarty Pass at an elevation of 1,021 feet near Aylen Lake Station.

After a ten-mile run through undeveloped country we arrive at Madawaska. This is the divisional point for the railway, complete with roundhouse, coal trestle, station and hotel. In our fifteen-minute stop, while our engine is changed, I am amazed at the amount of work which must have gone into carving out this town and these facilities from the surrounding bush country.

Shortly after leaving Madawaska, we pass another flagstop station and a railway spur leading off into the bush. I am informed that this is the Macauley Central Railway, a lumbering operation belonging to J.R. Booth. The railway is now following the course of the Madawaska River. The many stretches of rapids in this stretch of river make the trip very beautiful.

At 4:45 we arrive in Whitney, where we pass another railway leading into the woods. This is the Whitney and Opeongo Railway, which was built by the St. Anthony Lumber Company. We also pass a short spur leading to their mill.

As we leave Whitney, we cross a large bay of Long Lake before entering the woods ourselves. Before long we come back to the shore of Long Lake. This lake has many islands and inlets which, with the wooded shoreline, provide a beautiful view. We soon come upon Rock Lake, with its solid rock cliffs which drop right to water level and its many rocky islands which dot the surface of the lake.

At Rock Lake Station at the north end of the lake, we stop briefly to pick up a fur buyer with his bundle of furs. Train 65, the eastbound way freight from Depot Harbour, waits on the siding for us to clear the station at 5:10 p.m.

Three miles west of Rock Lake we cross over the Madawaska River at the south end of Whitefish Lake. I am informed by a fellow traveller that we have now entered Algonquin National Park. We stop partway up Whitefish Lake to take on water. We enter the woods again, roughly following the river, and pass Lake of Two Rivers. Entering the river valley at the west end of Two Rivers we begin to climb, cross the Madawaska once again and follow the north side of the valley. As we progress we see the river meandering through a grassy flood plain, dropping away from us as we climb. The hills close in on us, and once again the river is beside us with rushing rapids and waterfalls. We are nearing the top of a long grade when we swing out over the valley, crossing 50 feet above the river on a 300-foot long steel bridge. The view down the valley is spectacular.

We plunge in and out of the woods as we cross various bays of Cache Lake. We stop briefly at Algonquin Park Station to drop off passengers. One of the Park Rangers is standing by the station, swatting black flies, while checking for known poachers among the disembarking passengers. The Park Headquarters buildings can be seen as we leave the station. Leaving the lake behind, we roughly follow the Madawaska, not much more than a large stream by now. We cross it once more before coming upon Source Lake, the headwaters of this branch of the Madawaska River. Climbing over a slight divide, we cross Joe Lake and shortly arrive at Canoe Lake Station. A siding can be seen leading towards the Gilmour Company Lumber Mill, which was closed in 1900. There is a short delay as we take on water.

We cross Potter Creek and proceed to follow it west to Brule Lake. At Brule we start winding our way up a continuous grade for almost two miles. This brings us to the highest point on the line, 1,607 feet above sea level, where we enter the Georgian Bay watershed. We travel through a deep rock cut and out onto a high embankment overlooking Islet Lake. A further run through the woods brings us to Rainy Lake and our next water stop.

On leaving Rainy Lake we also leave Algonquin Park, wind our way over a small divide and continue on towards Scotia.

Eight miles after leaving Algonquin, I am startled to see the ground drop out from beneath us as we cross the Cashman Creek Bridge, 550 feet long and 76 feet tall.

We pause at Ravenworth Station before proceeding along the straightest section of railway we have encountered yet.   My attention is attracted by a disturbance at the far end of the coach. Apparently a youngster got stuck in the toilet, and the conductor was called upon to get him out.

Arriving at Kearney, we find Train 67, the eastbound mixed train out of Depot Harbour, waiting for our arrival. After a short halt both trains depart in opposite directions.

Five miles later we arrive at Scotia Junction. Here passengers transfer to the Grand Trunk Railway running from Toronto to North Bay. There are many sidings and facilities related to the exchange of freight between the two lines.

Leaving Scotia Junction we also leave behind the Algonquin Highlands, and enter a region of sandy hills, marshes and hardwood forests. The first siding we come to seems to signify the area we are travelling through. The sign simply says "Mud Lake".

Proceeding west, we come to Sprucedale, the first major town of any consequence west of Algonquin. I learn from a local teacher that this town is the local supply and educational centre. The town has both public and high schools, four grocery stores, a butcher shop and slaughterhouse. High school students from as far as Depot Harbour take the train to and from Sprucedale daily. Grocery orders from farmers and railway section crews along the line are sent out on the daily mixed trains.

While I talk with the teacher, we are travelling through a large marsh, and pass by the flagstop station at Whitehall.

Travelling on, we come to Bear Lake, another flagstop station. Here I say goodbye to the departing teacher, whose brother is waiting to take her home. The engine once again fills up with water. As we depart from Bear Lake, I notice a small sawmill and lumber yard near the tracks.

Passing through the community of Seguin Falls, we continue to Edgington at the north end of Maple Lake. On the outskirts of Edgington we pass a work train leaving the local gravel pits.

I learn that some of the passengers who boarded at Scotia are from Buffalo. They will be staying in Maple Lake for a few days before taking a canoe trip down through Muskoka.

After dropping them at the station in Maple Lake, we travel through a region of hardwood-covered hills and sparkling lakes. The railway seems to hug the hills halfway between the water and the sky. After passing James Bay Junction, where the five-mile James Bay Railway branches off for Parry Sound, we arrive at Rose Point. The twin-towered station overlooks the south channel of Parry Sound, with the beautiful Rose Point Hotel across the bay. Stopping here we allow passengers for Parry Sound to transfer to the ferry.

We continue across the swing bridge onto Parry Island, and ten minutes later arrive in Depot Harbour. The time is 9:00 p.m. The sun is going down over the bay, and I watch the sunset from my second-floor room in the Island Hotel.

Interior view of a typical smoking compartment on the Canada Atlantic Railway. Circa 1900. Public Archives Canada #C 26004

Interior view of a typical first class coach on the Canada Atlantic Railway. Circa 1900. Public Archives Canada #C 26001

View of the Canada Atlantic Station in Ottawa, 1895. Note the Government buildings in the background and the small company freight sheds to the left. Public Archives Canada #PA 8708

Typical first class passenger train passing through Elgin Street yards. Note the high level switch stands, stub type switches and crank type hand cars. Public Archives Canada #C 6317

Graham Bay
South March   *Typical flagstop stations.* W.G. Cole Collection CRHA

Carp Station, the first of the standard O.A. & P.S. stations. The freight shed could vary in size or location but the basic style remained the same. W.G. Cole Collection CRHA

Kinburn Station. Another view of the standard station. W.G. Cole Collection CRHA

In later years, Galetta was the site of a large steel water tank. W.G. Cole Collection CRHA

Arnprior Station, one of two stations of this style on the O.A. & P.S. The other is at Renfrew. W.G. Cole
Collection CRHA

The little flagstop at Goshen. W.G. Cole Collection CRHA

Renfrew Station. This is still in use by C.N.R. as a storage building. W.G. Cole Collection CRHA

Renfrew Junction. The Kingston and Pembroke Railway trackage is to the right of the building. The O.A. & P.S. is in the foreground. Public Archives Canada #PA 94781

The Eganville Station was mostly freight shed, with only a single-storey station building. W.G. Cole Collection CRHA

Golden Lake was the junction with the Pembroke Southern, which was leased by Canada Atlantic after 1899. W.G. Cole Collection CRHA

The stations at Douglas and Caldwell were non-standard and built to suit the size of community they served. W.G. Cole Collection CRHA

Early view of 4-4-0 #6 and train at Killaloe Station. Note link and pin coupler on flat car. Public Archives Canada #C 29160

Wilno was the site of Canada's first Polish community. W.G. Cole Collection CRHA

Barry's Bay Station. W.G. Cole Collection CRHA

The railway hotel peeks out from behind the station and freight shed at Madawaska. Algonquin Park
Museum #2303

A posed picture of the original five-stall roundhouse at Madawaska. Public Archives Canada #C23910

The fourteen-stall roundhouse built in 1907 at Madawaska. Algonquin Park Museum #2302

Coaling trestle at Madawaska, built 1906. Algonquin Park Museum #385

Water tower serving division point of Madawaska. Algonquin Park Museum #2300

Egan Estate Station at the junction with the Macauley Central Railway, a lumber branch line.
Algonquin Park Museum #603

The station at Whitney, location of the St. Anthony Lumber Company and junction with the Whitney and Opeongo, another lumber branch line. W.G. Cole Collection CRHA

The original station at Rock Lake. Algonquin Park Museum #2268

The second Rock Lake station. Algonquin Park Museum #2279

The Cache-Two Rivers trestle. The closing of this bridge in 1933 was the beginning of the end for the former O.A. & P.S. Railway. Public Archives Canada #PA 9347

Algonquin Park Station as it appeared after 1908. W.G. Cole Collection CRHA

View of the Headquarters Buildings at Algonquin Park, 1913. Public Archives Canada #PA 20593

View of Canoe Lake Station in 1915. Note siding at bottom left. One train would back in when a meet occurred at this station. Algonquin Park Museum #28

A canoe trip: disembarking from the train at Brule Lake Station. Algonquin Park Museum #4571

The sign at the summit grade. Algonquin Park Museum #2757

Scotia Junction Station 1910. Public Archives Canada #PA 21941

A view of the Junction looking north. The passenger car is on the O.A. & P.S. trackage. Algonquin Park Museum #362

Railway sidings. Possibly the trackage on the west side of Scotia Junction looking west. Public Archives Canada #C 11603

Sprucedale was the economic centre for the area west of Algonquin Park. W.G. Cole Collection CRHA

The stations west of Scotia varied in size according to the towns they served, as can be seen in these pictures of Whitehall and Bear Lake. W.G. Cole Collection

Edgington had three station agents providing 24-hour service, and therefore had the standard O.A.&P.S. style station. W.G. Cole Collection

The train operated by the Canada Atlantic from James Bay Junction to Parry Sound. Ontario Archives Acc. 10328, Tray 7 #19

Overall view of Rose Point looking towards Parry Island. Ontario Archives Acc. 10328, Tray 7 #35

Grand Trunk Station, Rose Point, Ont.

The twin towered station at Rose Point. Ontario Archives Acc. 10328, Tray 7 #25

ISLAND HOTEL

The Island Hotel in Depot Harbour. Ontario Archives Acc. 10328, Tray 5 #34

CHAPTER 4
THE RAILWAY AND THE WOODS

The area through which the O.A. & P.S. was constructed had long been associated with timber and lumber. The timber resources of the Ottawa River basin became of major importance in the Napoleonic Wars, when Great Britain's usual source of timber for shipbuilding, the countries around the Baltic Sea, were blockaded by the French. By the mid 1800's the square timber trade had reached its peak. Pine timbers two feet by two feet by forty feet were assembled in great rafts and floated down the Ottawa and St. Lawrence to Montreal, where the timbers were loaded on ships for Britain.

In the late 1800's, with the advent of iron or steel steamships and post Civil War construction in the United States, the emphasis on logging changed from the square timber trade to the sawlog industry, which provided sawn lumber to the markets in New England and Eastern Canada. The major transportation method was still the river, floating the logs to mill sites on the Ottawa and other major rivers. After drying, the lumber was then shipped by boat and barge to market areas.

The building of the Canada Atlantic Railway provided a more economical method of shipping lumber from Ottawa to New England. The O.A. & P.S., which was built as an extension to the C.A.R., increased lumbering possibilities, because it was constructed through vast areas of timberland which had not been settled or fully developed by the lumbering industry.

In 1894, with only 84 miles of the O.A. & P.S. opened for public traffic, 15,449 tons of lumber, 1,790 tons of grain, 3,186 tons of manufactured goods and 1,660 tons of assorted products were shipped. The dominance of wood products over other goods carried remained in effect throughout the construction years. Only with the completion of the O.A. & P.S. to Depot Harbour and its grain elevators was lumber challenged as the major commodity on the line.

In 1899 prior to the takeover by the Canada Atlantic, a total of 734,173 tons of freight were carried, of which lumber accounted for 269,092 tons, grain 260,636 tons and other goods a combined 204,445 tons.

The lumbering industry along the railway took many forms. In the farmland between Ottawa and Renfrew which had been settled prior to the building of the railway, the farmers were able to obtain a secondary income from cutting sawlogs on their woodlots or by working for large lumber companies during the winter months.

Large mills belonging to the McLachlan Lumber Company had been set up in Arnprior. These mills received logs from riverdrives on the Ottawa and, after completion of the railway, by rail from their timber limits north of Brule Lake. Lumber from the Pembroke area was shipped out to Golden Lake via the Pembroke Southern Railway, which was leased to the C.A.R.

The main shipper of wood products over the railway was the Booth Lumber Company. The O.A. & P.S. was built by J.R. Booth through the extensive timber limits near Madawaska, which were operated by the Booth Lumber Company. A short branch line, known as the Macaulay Central, was constructed in 1899 and connected with the O.A. & P.S. at Egan Estate Station, four and a half miles west of the division point at Madawaska. Locomotives belonging to the company operated the five mile line, bringing logs from the Macaulay Lake area into Madawaska. Regular O.A. & P.S. trains would then haul the loaded cars to Booth's mills in Ottawa. In later years the Macaulay Central was extended to Hardtack Lake, another eight to ten miles.

At the time that the O.A. & P.S. was constructed, there were various lumber companies operating in the Algonquin Park area.

The St. Anthony Lumber Company constructed a mill in Whitney in 1895, which was serviced by a three-quarter mile spur from the railway. In 1902 the lumber company constructed a 14.3 mile long branch line, the Whitney and Opeongo Railway, to transport logs from Sproule Bay on Lake Opeongo to its mill in Whitney. This railway remained in operation until 1926, using a switching engine owned by the lumber company. Finished lumber was shipped out over the trackage of the O.A. & P.S.

The Gilmour Company held the timber limits around Canoe Lake in Algonquin Park. In 1894 it started a log drive which would take two years to reach its mill in Trenton. The logs started in Algonquin Park, were floated down the Oxtongue River to Lake of Bays and transferred to the headwaters of the Trent River at Raven Lake. To get over the height of land between the two river systems, the Gilmour Company constructed the Dorset Tramway, a continuously operated steam-powered jack ladder with timberslides for the downhill trip. By the time the logs reached the mill a large portion were unusable, because of rot and damage. As a result, in 1896 the Gilmour Company set up a mill and other company buildings at Mowat, near the north end of Canoe Lake on Potter Creek. The O.A. & P.S. built a spur and sidings eventually totalling eleven miles in length, to service these facilities and those of other lumber companies which used this site.

The Gilmour Company closed its operation at Canoe Lake in 1900, after only four years of operations. The company had employed 600 men at this site.

Prior to 1900, only pine was cut in Algonquin Park. An amendment to The Parks Act permitted the cutting of spruce, hemlock, birch, cedar, black ash and tamarack. In 1913 a further amendment negotiated by J.R. Booth, allowing lumber companies to negotiate what species of tree they would cut, opened the way for continuous lumbering in Algonquin Park. In the first half of this century, additional mills were operated in Algonquin Park by various lumber companies.

A small temporary community grew up at Brule Lake, to house local mill workers. Another, at Mowat on Canoe Lake, housed workers for the Gilmour Company and later the Canoe Lake and Omanique Lumber Companies.

The McRae Lumber Company, which still cuts lumber in the Algonquin area, had two mills serviced by the railway. The first mill was at the community of Belwood on Galeairy Lake (formerly Long Lake), west of Whitney. Train loads of sawlogs were delivered to this mill to supplement logs hauled over tote-roads owned by the company.

In the early 1930's, the McRae mill was moved to Lake of Two Rivers. After the closure of the Cache-Two Rivers trestle in 1933, due to weakened foundations caused by an unexpected flood, the McRae mill was the furthest west that freight trains from Ottawa reached. Passenger travel stopped at Rock Lake. McRae's did operate rail speeders for personnel wishing to travel to Rock Lake or beyond.

As the trestle was unsafe for heavier railway equipment, arrangements were made for an automobile on flanged wheels to operate over this same stretch between Cache Lake (Algonquin Park Station) and Madawaska. This was to provide through service for passengers from Depot Harbour to Ottawa until the rails on the bridge were taken up in 1940.

The McRae's mill at Two Rivers was moved to Rock Lake in 1942, and rail service was discontinued west of Rock Lake Station.

As automotive technology developed better trucks, the trucking industry became more useful to lumber companies, and the railway in Algonquin ceased to be used to transport logs and lumber.

The western portion of the O.A. & P.S. between Scotia Junction and Depot Harbour passed through country filled with hardwood forests. The economy of the area was based on a combination of farming and lumbering. The local farmer could produce little more than they required for their families. Occasionally they could ship livestock to markets, or to the slaughterhouse in Sprucedale, to obtain money for supplies that they could not grow. Their main income came from winter lumbering, as every property had large acreages of hardwood woodlots.

These farmer-lumbermen would selectively cut the best trees over 12 inches in diameter and haul them either to the railway for loading onto flatcars or to a local mill for cutting. Hauling was primarily done in the winter, as the frozen lakes provided an easier access route than the tote-roads over the hills. On a clear winter day, residents of Edgington could often see up to thirty teams of horses hauling logs across Maple Lake, some coming from 15 to 20 miles away.

Although the logs were shipped primarily in the winter, cut lumber was shipped year round. The local mills would stockpile logs in the winter for summer production. Cut lumber would also be stacked to dry at the mill site until it was required.

Lumber mills close to the railway, such as the mill at Bear lake, had sidings into their lumber yards. Other mills further from the railway had other arrangements. Some would haul the lumber in winter to the closest railway siding for storage and shipment.

The owners of the mill at Maple Lake, situated a mile from the station, built a narrow gauge railway to transport the lumber to the sidings for transfer to the O.A. & P.S.

Crews of men would be kept busy loading lumber trains year round. Occasional special loads would be shipped. Trainloads of oak square timber, two feet by two feet by forty feet, were shipped once every couple of years. They could not be shipped more often because of the difficulty in transporting timber of this size to the railway. Another type of special load was hardwood flats. These boards, four inches thick and 12 to 18 inches wide with bark edges, were shipped to hardwood flooring manufacturers. The flooring companies would use multi-bladed saws to cut the flats into one by four inch flooring.

Many of the sawlogs were destined for the Oakville Basket Works, which manufactured baskets and boxes. The buyers for this company would travel from depot to depot, buying only the best logs from the farmers.

The remainder of the logs were often sold to the Standard Chemical Company in South River. It used them to produce charcoal, wood alcohol and acetylene. In later years Standard Chemical hired crews of men to cut cordwood from woodlots purchased from farmers and other landowners. This resulted in the demise of the hardwood lumber industry in the area, as they cut down trees as small as three to four inches in diameter. The remaining trees would require decades to again reach marketable size. This factor, along with the closing of the O.A. & P.S. trackage in 1952, created a massive setback to the economy of this area.

The final source of lumber or sawlogs shipped on the trackage of the O.A. & P.S. came from Georgian Bay. Various lumber mills shipped their products by water to Depot Harbour for transfer to the railway. This practice did not last too many years, as the construction of the Canadian Northern and Canadian Pacific Railways through the area supplied alternative, less expensive transportation.

The O.A. & P.S. owed its beginnings to the lumber industry. It helped to develop a large portion of Ontario and encouraged the further development of the Canadian lumber industry. The lumbering remains but the railway is gone. This is ever the story of the railway and the woods.

Large raft of square timber, belonging to J.R. Booth, in the Ottawa River. Public Archives Canada #C 6096

Loading sawn lumber onto barges for shipment down the Ottawa River. Public Archives Canada #PA 9298

J.R. Booth's lumber camp along the Macauley Central. Public Archives Canada #PA 120336

Loading logs on the Macauley Central. Public Archives Canada #PA 120337

Canada Atlantic Locomotive 681 removing a train of logs from the Macauley Central Branch. Public Archives Canada #PA 120341

In 1924 a special train of waney timbers (partially squared pine) was shipped out over Canadian National from the Macauley Central. This was the last pine shipment from Algonquin Park. Algonquin Park Museum#1049

A view of the St. Anthony Lumber Company mill at Whitney. Algonquin Park Museum #2318

Loading logs at Sproule Bay on the Whitney and Opeongo Railway. Algonquin Park Museum #3298

A switching engine used at Whitney by the lumber company. Algonquin Park Museum #2317

The Canoe Lake Lumber Company as it appeared in 1922. It was located at the former site of the Gilmour Lumber Company on Canoe Lake. Algonquin Park Musuem#3450

A view of the Omanique Lumber Company Mill built at the former site of the Canoe Lake and Gilmour Mills. Note the special railway cars used for the sorting and stacking of lumber. Algonquin Park Museum #1272

End view of the Brule Lake Mill. 1930. Algonquin Park Museum #1311

Lumber stacks and sidings at Brule in 1930. Note the stub switch. Algonquin Park Museum #1308

The McRae Mill at Belwood on Galeairy Lake. Algonquin Park Museum #2708

A general view of McRae's Mill at Lake of Two Rivers. Algonquin Park Museum #1283

A typical gas speeder at Lake of Two Rivers. Algonquin Park Museum #2774

This shows the method used to unload logs at their destination. This view taken in Ottawa in 1925. Public Archives Canada #PA 86976

A view taken from the grain elevator at Depot Harbour. Note the transhipment of lumber taking place.
Ontario Archive Acc. 10328 Tray 5, Photo #28

CHAPTER 5
TOURISM AND THE RAILWAY

"Two million acres of fish and game preserve — a woodland paradise for the fisherman and camper 2,000 feet above sea level.

ALGONQUIN NATIONAL PARK OF ONTARIO

Speckled trout, salmon trout and black bass abound in the 1,200 lakes and rivers of this vast territory. Camp out and rough it; or, if you prefer, good hotel accommodations make it an ideal summering place for tourists."

Thus it was that the Grand Trunk Railway system started an advertisement campaign to attract tourists to Algonquin Park.

When the Grand Trunk took over the operations of the Canada Atlantic Railway system in 1905, there was little justification for the through passenger trains operated "daily except Sunday" from Ottawa to Depot Harbour. Although the Government had started to lease land for summer residences that year, and though the local people travelled through the Park, most of the passenger traffic occurred from Ottawa to Montreal and Ottawa to Madawaska.

To encourage the use of the railway into Algonquin Park, the Grand Trunk opened a lodge in 1908 called Highland Inn. In its first season of operation, Highland Inn consisted of a dining hall and a series of tents with wooden platform floors. These were situated on the hillside above the railway at Algonquin Park Station on Cache Lake, which was also the location of the Park Headquarters buildings.

In the same year the Hotel Algonquin was constructed at Joe Lake, and Northway Lodge, the first of many youth camps to be operated in Algonquin Park, was started at Cache Lake. Both of these were private enterprises unrelated to the railway.

The advertising campaign was obviously a success, because the Grand Trunk expanded its facilities at Highland Inn. In 1911 two more youth camps started up, Camp Ahmeek on Lady Joe Lake and Camp Minnewawa at Lake of Two Rivers.

The year 1913 was a very busy one for tourism in the Park. Highland Inn now contained over 75 guest rooms. The Grand Trunk constructed two further rustic camps affiliated with Highland Inn. They were Camp Nominigan on Smoke Lake and Camp Minnesing on Burnt Island Lake. These two lodges were reached by stagecoach from Highland Inn or by canoe. The railway offered special packages for guests at Highland Inn. The railway would transport guests and their canoes from Cache Lake to Canoe Lake Station. The guests would paddle through Canoe Lake into Smoke Lake, stay overnight at Nominigan, and finish their canoe trip to Highland Inn the next day. Highland Inn had complete outfitting facilities and hired guides for the use of its patrons, at a charge, of course.

In the same year Mr. and Mrs. Shannon Fraser opened Mowat Lodge using a building previously owned by the Gilmour Lumber Company.

Despite the outbreak of war in 1914, another youth camp, Camp Pathfinder, was opened on Source Lake. Algonquin Park had become a very popular place for vacationers.

The Twenties brought many changed to the tourist facilities in Algonquin Park. Mowat Lodge burned down, and was rebuilt on another site. Camp Ahmek for boys was started by Taylor Stratten on Canoe Lake. Camp Ahmeek on Lady Joe Lake was closed after only eleven years.

In 1923, with the takeover of the Grand Trunk by Canadian National Railways, Minnesing Lodge was sold. It was subsequently used for religious seminars. Highland Inn was quite popular, holding special events such as regattas and dances on regular basis for its patrons. Taking advantage of these activities, Bartlett Lodge was opened up across the lake from Highland Inn.

The year 1924 saw the founding of Camp Wopomeo on Canoe Lake, a girls' camp operated by Mrs. Taylor Statten. This was followed by Camp Tanamakoon on White Lake one season later. White Lake was later renamed Tanamakoon Lake.

The third property which had been built by the Grand Trunk, Nominigan Lodge, suffered a setback when the guest cabins burned down in 1926. Nominigan was sold five years later for use as a summer residence.

Up until this time the railway had been greatly involved with the tourism, because it was the only form of reliable transport to the Park. With the Depression, this began to change. In 1933 two major events occurred which would result in the demise of the railway. The Government began the construction of Highway 60 through the Park, as a make-work project. This undertaking would not have been of great importance to the railway, had not one of its steel trestles been condemned.

The foundations of the trestle between Cache Lake and Lake of Two Rivers had been weakened by an unexpected flood. The C.N.R., which also owned the ex-Canadian Northern Railway trackage between Ottawa and North Bay, did not consider the repair of the bridge very important. Not wishing to spend money on this repair itself, the C.N.R. applied to the Government for funds to repair or replace the bridge.

The Government, already spending money on Highway 60 which roughly paralleled the railway, turned down the railway's request, on the grounds that two transportation routes were not required to maintain the economy of the Algonquin Park area.

Ironically, although the Government was correct about Algonquin Park's economy and tourism continued to grow and more camps and lodges were set up, the closure of the Cache-Two Rivers bridge was indirectly responsible for the destruction of the economy of the communities on the western portion of the O.A. & P.S.

The railway no longer offered the shortest route between the Upper Great Lakes and New England, so grain and package goods were re-routed to ports other than Depot Harbour. Coal was still shipped over the line until it was de-emphasized as a heating fuel. Trains became less frequent and eventually, in 1952, the railway between Scotia and South Parry, near Depot Harbour, was closed.

The railway into Algonquin Park from the west remained in use until 1959. Running primarily on weekends, it provided service to the many cottagers using the Park, as well as the camps and lodges.

In 1957 the two largest lodges in the Park, Highland Inn and Hotel Algonquin, were sold to the Government and taken down. The railway was no longer necessary, as the growing number of campers were able to drive to the public campsites throughout Algonquin.

The last train into Algonquin Park was a special run in 1959. Camp Tanamakoon requested a train to move the girls at the camp out at the end of the summer. Shortly after this special train was run, the rails were taken up.

Not all of the tourist activities occurred in Algonquin Park; there were small hotels in Sprucedale and Maple Lake, as well as a large hotel at Rose Point.

The hotel in Sprucedale was not really tourist-related, as the area was more business-oriented. The town had two schools, four grocery stores, a butcher shop and a bank, and was the economic centre of the region.

Maple Lake, on the other hand, could boast of the "Buffalo Flyer". Tourists from New York and Pennsylvania would travel via Buffalo over the Grand Trunk Railway to Maple Lake. They would stay overnight, or two or three nights, before taking a stagecoach to another hotel on Lake Joseph. Here they would embark on canoe trips which would end in Gravenhurst or Washago, where they would board the train for their return trip home.

The Maple Lake Hotel was also popular with retired railway men, who would come from the States, using their railway passes, and stay for a week or two of fishing.

The Rose Point Hotel was another lodge offering regattas and other special events, much like Highland Inn. It was situated across the bay from the station at Rose Point, looking out toward Parry Sound. It was reached by a timber causeway from the station, or by boat from the town of Parry Sound. With the passing of the railway it became more difficult to reach the Rose Point Hotel, and it became less popular. Today it has been replaced by a marina catering to the cottagers who inhabit the 30,000 islands of Georgian Bay.

Thus it was that the O.A. & P.S. Railway contributed greatly to the development of Algonquin Park as a tourist attraction during the years it was operated by the Grand Trunk. It is ironic that today the O.A. & P.S. itself, if it were still running, would be a main attraction for tourists.

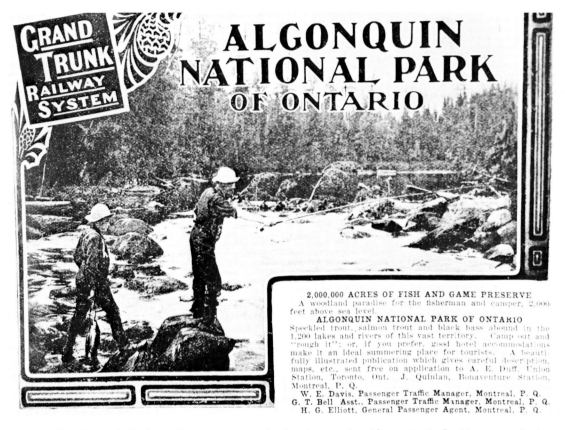

Grand Trunk Railway System promotional advertisement for Algonquin Park. Algonquin Park Museum #2667

Highland Inn as it appeared in its first summer of operation. Algonquin Park Museum #2864

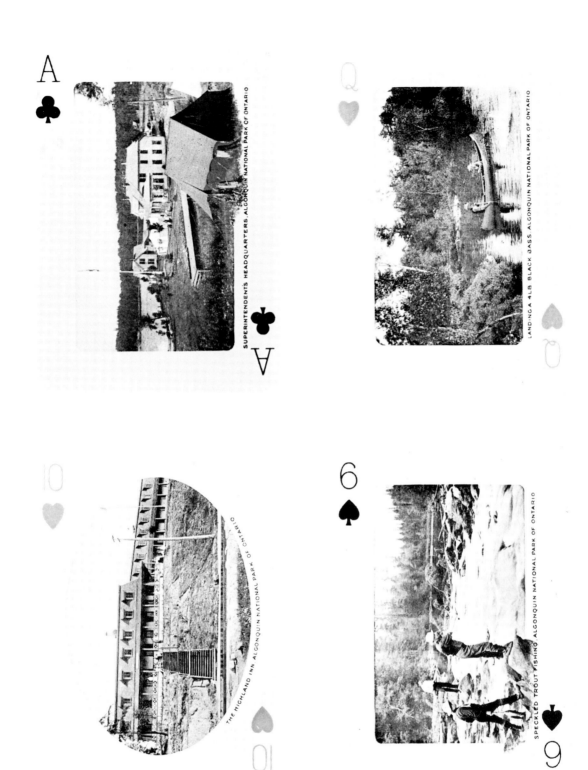

To help promote tourism in general, the Grand Trunk issued playing cards showing fifty-two views in Eastern Canada. The cards shown related to points along the O.A. & P.S. Railway. J.D.M. Phillips Collection

A frontal view of the Hotel Algonquin as it appeared in 1922. Algonquin Park Museum #620

View of Smoke Lake showing Nominigan Camp. Public Archives Canada #PA 48738

Highland Inn as it appeared in 1913. Public Archives Canada #C 56135

Stage to Nominigan passing under the railway. Algonquin Park Museum #474

Camp Minnesing on Burnt Island Lake. Algonquin Park Museum #2259

A view of Highland Inn during the winter of 1920. Public Archives Canada #PA 84004

Bartlett Lodge, constructed in 1923. Algonquin Park Museum #1136

The main lodge of Nominigan Camp as it appeared in 1936. Algonquin Park Museum #482

The Cache-Two Rivers trestle. The closing of this bridge in 1933 caused the decline of this railway as an important transportation route. Algonquin Park Museum #1289

A weekend train at Highland Inn. After 1933 this was as far as the trains ran into Algonquin Park. Here they would be turned and return to the mainline at Scotia Junction. Algonquin Park Museum #747

The Hotel Algonquin on the hill above Joe Lake Station. Algonquin Park Museum #183

The last train into Algonquin Park in 1959. It was hauled by two C.N.R. diesel switchers. Algonquin Park Museum #1476

A view across the Bay from the Rose Point Station. The large building is the Rose Point Hotel. Ontario Archives Acc. 10328, Tray 7 #28

The Rose Point Hotel. Ontario Archives Acc. 10328, Tray 7 #26

CHAPTER 6
DEPOT HARBOUR—THE RAILWAY TOWN

During the construction of the Ottawa Arnprior and Parry Sound Colonization Railways, a decison was made which had a great effect on the lives of many people.

When looking at potential sites for the terminus of the railway, J.R. Booth looked beyond the obvious location at the town of Parry Sound. Although Parry Sound offered a resident work force and sufficient dock space, it had two major disadvantages, in his opinion. He realized that the harbour facilities, located at a river mouth, would require periodic dredging. He also was put off by the amount of money requested by Parry Sound for the dock space he would require. Both of these factors would have been overlooked and the railway built into Parry Sound, had not the best natural harbour in the Great Lakes existed only a few miles away on Parry Island.

Thus it was that the site of Depot Harbour was chosen as the terminus of the O.A. & P.S. An entire town large enough for three hundred people was constructed in 1897 on land leased from the Indian Reservation on Parry Island. The railway constructed 89 single and double family dwellings, a boarding house for transient employees, the town hall, post office, general store and butcher shop, as well as those buildings required by the railway itself.

As with other aspects of the O.A. & P.S., the Depot Harbour facilities were constructed on a grand scale in anticipation of a great deal of traffic. The grain elevators when originally constructed were designed to hold one million bushels of grain; an extension completed in 1907 added another million bushels capacity. When it is considered that by 1910 one hundred to one hundred and twenty carloads of grain were shipped daily, this would seem quite adequate, yet often three or four ships were tied up waiting to be unloaded.

The freight sheds were also built on a large scale. They were built on pilings and rubble in thirty feet of water. A twenty-three hundred foot long, double track trestle was constructed to reach them. The two freight sheds themselves were enormous, being sixteen feet high, eighty feet wide, and six hundred and seven hundred feet long respectively. An additional seven thousand eight hundred square feet of platform was constructed. It was possible for four lake steamers carrying package freight to tie up at the freight sheds at the same time.

Among the major commodities transferred through the freight sheds were processed grain goods; flour, livestock feeds, etc. This was all unloaded by men with two-wheeled hand carts, twelve bags to a load. When the ships first tied up and were low in the water, it would take three men to move a load up the plank to the shed platform. As the ship emptied, it would rise in the water until one man could take the load down the plank to the shed platform.

Manufactured goods and packages from the East would be loaded onto the steamers for the return trip to the Great Lakes ports from which they came. The shipment of package goods over the railway accounted for over one hundred and twenty-five carloads a day by 1910. Combined with the grain shipments, this resulted in an average of one train every twenty minutes.

The number of ships which began using Depot Harbour as a terminal was not left to chance. In 1899, after completing the railway, J.R. Booth set up the Canada Atlantic Transit Company and the Canada Atlantic Transit Company of the United States, steamship lines primarily serving the lake ports of Fort William, Ontario and Duluth, Minnesota, with provision to serve other Canadian and American ports in the Great Lakes. A total of seven ships were operated at one time or another by these companies. They were, in order of purchase, S.S. Newond, S.S. Ottawa, S.S. George Orr, S.S. Kearsage, S.S. Arthur Orr, S.S. Canatco and the S.S. Delwarnic. The last four ships were still in use until the middle of the Second World War. There was no service after the war and the charters of both companies lapsed by 1950.

Other steamship lines also used Depot Harbour as a terminus, as the O.A. & P.S. had shortened the distance to Montreal by 800 miles. Prior to the construction of the O.A. & P.S., grain travelled by freighter to Montreal via Lakes Erie and Ontario, a much longer and more expensive route.

By 1911 the population of Depot Harbour had risen to over six hundred, rivalling Parry Sound as the main centre of the area.

The First World War had little effect on the town other than to make it busier, if that were possible. In the winter of 1915 fifteen ships of grain for the war effort were tied up awaiting unloading. When space became available in the elevators to hold the grain, crews of men would cut a path through the ice with crosscut saws, to enable a ship to move up to the dock for unloading.

To the people of Depot Harbour, the railway was everything. You worked for the railway. You travelled by railway to Sprucedale if you went to high school. All connections with the outside were by railway or boat. The railway was the only employer in town, although you did have your choice of the elevators, the sheds, the coal docks, the ice house, the machine shop and roundhouse or the railway crew itself. Everything except recreation, if you had time, revolved around the railway.

In the summer months, when shipping was at its height, the elevators and sheds would run twelve to eighteen hours a day while ships were in port, unless it was a Sunday, when no trains operated.

Life continued this way with only minor changes resulting from the takeover of the Grand Trunk by Canadian National Railways in 1923. In 1933 an event occurred one hundred miles from Depot Harbour which would mean the end for the town.

An unexpected flood, possibly caused by a broken beaver dam, weakened the foundations of the Cache-Two Rivers trestle. The Government refused the C.N.R.'s request for funds to replace or repair the bridge. The Government at this time was undertaking the construction of Highway 60 as a Depression relief measure, and did not feel that two transportation routes through the same area were required. It also reasoned that the C.N.R. had an alternate route from Ottawa to the Great Lakes via the ex-Canadian Northern line to North Bay and that two routes were not required.

With the closing of this bridge, the route through Depot Harbour ceased to be the shortest route to New England. Grain shipments were re-routed through North Bay or other ports serviced by railway. Package freight still continued, as did coal shipments.

During the last half of World War Two the grain elevators and freight sheds were used for the storage of cordite explosive. In the summer of 1945 the grain elevators were gradually being torn down, although still being used to store cordite. On the evening of the victory over Japan, two men were seen running from the elevators just prior to flames being spotted. The explosion and the fire which followed could be seen in Parry Sound, four miles away. Some people were able to read newspapers at midnight on the main street.

Sparks from the elevators drifted across the harbour and ignited the freight sheds, which also contained cordite, and wool. As the windows in the sheds were open, the cordite fizzled rather than exploded. Both sheds burned down to the waterline.

This ended any hope of re-activating the packaged goods shipments through Depot Harbour. All that remained of the elevators was a four-foot high pile of hand-made nails and iron rods which had held together the wooden planks from which the elevators had been made.

To clear the dock space, this pile of iron was shoved into the harbour by a bulldozer.

The Century Coal Company took over the dock space where the elevators had been. The pond, which to this time had separated the dock from the shoreline, was filled in and used as a base for a large stockpile of coal. This trans-shipment of coal continued from 1945 until 1951, when coal became less important as a fuel. Further shipment of coal went directly by ship to steel companies and generating stations.

With the closing of the Century Coal facilities, there was no further need for a community at Depot Harbour. In 1952 the trackage between Scotia Junction and James Bay Junction was torn up. Over the next few years the buildings in Depot Harbour were sold by the railway for the lumber from which they were built.

In 1959 the National Steel Company of Canada began to use the facilities of Depot Harbour for trans-shipment of Northern Ontario iron ore to lake steamers for delivery to Hamilton, etc. By this time the community of Depot Harbour had almost disappeared, and steel company workers commuted from Parry Sound. The steel company operations continued until the fall of 1979, when the mine from which the ore came closed down. The equipment waits patiently for the next train.

In 1978 a small fertilizer company called Pot-Cal set up a small plant at Depot Harbour, only to be bankrupt within two years.

The townsite today is covered with brush. Only one of the original buildings is left, now being used as a cottage. An occasional foundation or a collapsed building gives evidence of a town that once was, and the concrete steps no longer lead to the Roman Catholic church.

The tracks still go to the harbour, but only as a branch line. The concrete walls of the roundhouse stand silently among the trees, the last testament to the great times of the past.

Depot Harbour is a true ghost town. There is nothing left to show that over three generations of people lived here. Depot Harbour now exists only as a memory of former inhabitants, which still number in the hundreds.

This view of the town was taken from the top of the elevators. Note the two styles of dwellings, peaked roof single-family style and flat roof double-family style. The original roundhouse is visible at centre right.
Ontario Archives Acc. 10328, Tray 5 #16

A typical "closet" or outhouse of the type built by the railway.
Dave Thomas Collection

The local post office and general store. Ontario Archives Acc. 10328, Tray 5 #42

An early view of the grain elevators. The unloading facilities for coal can also be seen beyond the elevators.
Ontario Archives Acc. 10328, Tray 5 #18

Another view of the coal transfer facilities at Depot Harbour. Public Archives Canada #PA 20601

A view of the completed elevators. They had a capacity of two million bushels. Ontario Archives Acc. 10328, Tray 5 #28

A rear view of the elevators, showing the railcar loading facilities.
Dave Thomas Collection

This view shows the ample siding space and equipment needed at Depot Harbour. Ontario Archives
Acc. 10328, Tray 5 #45

Canada Atlantic Transit Company of the U.S. Steamship Arthur Orr tied up at the freight shed. Dave Thomas Collection

This view of the elevators shows the power house. A continuous rope ran from here to and throughout the elevators, powering all functions within the building. Dave Thomas Collection

The ice crews outside the ice house. Dave Thomas Collection

The churches were built by the people of Depot Harbour. Ontario Archives Acc. 10328, Tray 5 #32

To many youngsters the day's activities centred around this building — the school. Ontario Archives
Acc. 10328, Tray 5 #29

This pile of twisted metal was all that remained of the elevators after the fire. Dave Thomas Collection

From 1959 through 1979 the National Steel Company of Canada used Depot Harbour as a transfer point for Northern Ontario ore. Dave Thomas Collection

A train load of empties crossing the Rose Point bridge. Dave Thomas Collection

Empty windows peek out of the trees. This was part of the roundhouse back wall. Author's Collection

CHAPTER 7
THE RAILWAY AS IT IS TODAY

It is hard to believe today that over half of the O.A. & P.S., which was conceived and constructed by one man, and which became so important to the economy and people of the area through which it passed, has now become only a memory.

To make a trip from Ottawa to Depot Harbour today would require many forms of transportation.

From Ottawa to Barry's Bay you can still travel in comfort behind a beautiful steam locomotive, but only on the July First weekend, when ex-Canadian Pacific Railway Locomotive #1201 runs an excursion. Occasional excursions hosted by the Bytown Railway Society are also run over this trackage. The remaining freight service is run three times a week if required, and the section crew based in Renfrew patrols the line on a regular basis.

Only three stations still exist on the railway. These are Renfrew, used by the railway for storage, Eganville, recently leased to a private interest, and Barry's Bay, which has been fully restored and is in use by the Senior Citizens.

The railway can be travelled by handcar from Barry's Bay as far as Whitney — provided, that is, that you clear out all the inch and a half saplings from between the rails. The ruins of the roundhouse at Madawaska stand silently beside a ballpark.

At Whitney you must start to walk, or if you wait until winter you can travel the next fifteen miles by cross country skis. A one-mile section of this stretch of right of way is also used on the Booth Rock Trail, a self-conducted nature and history trail maintained by the Ministry of Natural Resources. At the north end of Rock Lake the old roadbed is used as the access road to Rock Lake campgrounds and to the grounds of the McRae Lumber Company mill.

From the north end of Lake of Two Rivers, the underbrush closes in as you walk along the old roadbed. The occasional rotting tie still lies in place. You soon come to old masonry abutments, all that is left of the third crossing over the Madawaska. By skirting the south shore of the river, and crossing at the shallow rapids nearby, you can reach the railway again.

The roadbed continues in an overgrown state as you climb up the side of the valley. Suddenly you come across a section of the railway which was used as an access road to the Cache Lake Dam. This road turns off just before you reach the site of the Cache-Two Rivers trestle. The masonry piers can be seen marching down one side of the valley and up the other.

To reach the other side you will need hip boots, or a towel to dry your feet, to cross the river, and determination to climb up the other side of the valley.

A short walk through rock cuts and spruce forests brings you to a long trestle. It is best to take to a boat for a half mile or so, as this trestle, and another one hundred yards further along, are no longer safe to cross.

Back on the right of way, you find that the local cottagers use this section as a footpath to and from the parking lot at the former site of Algonquin Park Station.

As you approach the far side of the parking lot, a concrete platform appears in a thick growth of Scotch pine. This is the station platform that stretched along the hillside below Highland Inn. The site of the Inn itself is totally covered by the pines.

The railway, as it leaves Cache Lake, travels through a few rock cuts before crossing Highway 60. You would be advised to wear rubber boots, as the drainage ditches have filled up over the years and the right of way is now quite wet — a lovely place for mosquitoes to propagate.

The right of way starts to rise, offering you a beautiful view of the Madawaska River, before you come to Source Lake on the right.

At the west end of Source Lake you walk along the right of way, sometimes used as a logging road, until you reach a washed-out embankment north of Brule Lake.

Walking down the hillside, you come across a rusted set of railway wheels left over from an early derailment.

As you climb the other side of the washout, the remains of pilings can be seen sticking out of the embankment. This is evidence of one of the many temporary trestles once built on the line.

From here to Rainy Lake is a good walk, through the summit rock cut, and over the fifty foot high embankment at Islet Lake. At the west end of Rainy Lake you greet the Park ranger before entering a car for the trip to Kearney along the right of way, now an access road for Algonquin Park.

The right of way from Kearney to Scotia is passable by truck, but not recommended, as it has had no grading or roadwork done since the tracks were removed in 1975.

At Scotia Junction, no more than a siding on the Toronto-North Bay line now, you must make a detour, as the railway west of here is nothing more than a line of alders running through marsh and bog for the next few miles and impassable by vehicle or by foot.

At Fern Glen you return to the right of way, and find it marked as the Seguin Trail, maintained by the Ministry of Natural Resources. From here to Highway 69 south of Parry Sound the old railway has been designated as a snowmobile trail.

The Seguin Trail is best travelled in the winter. Although some sections are passable by truck, you will often come upon a bridge which is not strong enough or too narrow to cross. This usually occurs when you are half a mile out into a marsh on an embankment with no place to turn, or some equally difficult spot. Walking further along such stretches would only invite lots of insect bites. As for points of interest along this stretch, there are few. It is mostly water, sand, rock and scrub bush for the first twenty-five miles.

Further along, you pass into hardwood forests, with the occasional stream running across the right of way. The roadbed is often used as a road by hunters and local cottagers. It travels through deep rock cuts and hugs the side of lakes and hills as it approaches Highway 69.

On the west side of the highway, the right of way is again covered with alders. It turns north, paralleling the highway to James Bay Junction.

A well-kept trestle indicates that this part of the railway was recently used. Although no ore trains travel this route any more, the trackage from the Junction to Rose Point and Depot Harbour is still maintained and sometimes used as sidings for surplus equipment.

The swing bridge at Rose Point is still opened once a day to allow the 30,000 Islands cruise ship to pass, but is normally closed, because it is also the road access to Parry Island.

At Depot Harbour the transfer facilities of the Steel Company of Canada lie silent. Only one of the company-built houses of 1899 remains.

The once-proud walls of the eleven-stall roundhouse act as a silent sentinel over this ghost of a town and pale shadow of a once-great railway.

Ex-C.P.R. Locomotive #1201 on excursion service. R. Beaumont photo

Renfrew Station as it appeared October 1980. This is still being used by the railway, but only as storage space.

Renfrew Junction. Although most of the Kingston and Pembroke is long gone, this track remains as an interchange betwen C.N.R. and C.P.R.

Eganville Station in October 1980. This station has recently been leased to a private concern.

Barry's Bay Station. Now used by Senior Citizens as a meeting place. R. Beaumont photo

The water tower stands empty at Barry's Bay.

This magnificent bridge can be seen from Highway 60 as you enter Madawaska from the east.

The remains of the roundhouse at Madawaska can also be seen from the highway.

This trestle just west of Whitney now has a new decking for use by cross country skiers.

Typical scene on the right of way between Lake of Two Rivers and Algonquin Park Station.

One of the two long trestles in Cache Lake. The end sections of these trestles have now started to collapse. This is the site of a former trestle type culvert.

Only the concrete platform remains visible to show the site of Highland Inn.

North from Highway 60 the right of way follows the Madawaska River, seen here on the left.

This bridge at Potter Creek is now used as part of an access road by cottagers and Ministry of Natural Resources personnel.

This arch bar railway truck can be found north of Brule Lake, where the embankment has been washed out.

The old railway from Fern Glen to Highway 69 is now designated as the Seguin Trail for snowmobile usage.

This trestle is still in use as part of the switchback required to enter the Depot Harbour branch

The Rose Point swing bridge, normally closed, is still in operating condition and opened at least once a day during the summer.

CHAPTER 8
THE EQUIPMENT OF THE O.A.&P.S.

During the construction years 1893-1896, the equipment used on the O.A. & P.S. was leased from the Canada Atlantic. These locomotives were mostly secondhand 4-4-0 types built by various manufacturers. The Canada Atlantic at this time also owned five 2-6-0 type engines built by Rhode Island in 1886/87 and seven 4-4-0 type engines built by Baldwin between 1893 and 1896. These were used mostly on the service between Ottawa and Vermont, and in 1897 on the O.A. & P.S.

In 1898, with the operations in full swing, two sets of locomotives were delivered to the O.A. & P.S., ten of the 4-6-0 type, numbers 629 to 638, and six of the 2-8-0 type number 690 to 695. An additional eight locomotives of the 2-8-0 type numbers 696 to 703 were delivered the following year. All of these locomotives were Baldwin built, Vauclain compound type. All of the above locomotives were used for freight service.

Two 4-4-2 Atlantic type locomotives were also purchased from Baldwin in 1899 for use in fast passenger service between Ottawa and Madawaska.

The following is an excerpt from the June 1899 "Railway and Shipping World", giving details of these engines.

Canada

Atlantic

Equipment

Excerpt from
The Railway & Shipping World
June 1899

ATLANTIC
FOR FAST PASSENGER SERVICE.

Cylinders.—Diameter (high pressure)	13 in.
" " (low pressure)	22 in.
" Stroke	26 in.
" Valve	Balanced Piston
Boiler.—Diameter	60 in.
" Thickness of Sheets	$^{11}/_{16}$ in.
" Working Pressure	200
" Fuel	Soft Coal
Firebox.—Material	Steel
" Length	103 $^3/_{16}$ in
" Width	42$^1/_8$ in.
" Depth	F., 71½ in.; B., 69 in.
" Thickness of Sheets, sides	$^5/_{16}$ in.
" " back	$^5/_{16}$ in.
" " crown	$^3/_8$ in.
" " tube	½ in.
Tubes.—Number	262
" Diameter	2 in.
" Length	15 ft.
Driving Wheels.—Diameter Outside	78 in.
" " of Centre	72 in.
" Journals	8x12 in.
Engine Truck Wheels.—Diameter	36 in.
" Journals	5½x10 in.
Trailing Wheels.—Diameter	54 in.
" Journals	8x12 in.
Wheel Base.—Driving	6 ft. 9 in.
" Total Engine	25 ft. 6 in.
" Rigid	13 ft. 9 in.
Tender.—Diameter of Wheels	36 in.
" Journals	5x9 in.
" Tank Capacity	6,000 gals.

10-WHEELER
FOR FREIGHT SERVICE.

Cylinders.—Diameter (high pressure) .... 14 in.
"   "   (low pressure) .... 24 in.
"   Stroke .... 26 in.
"   Valve .... Balanced Piston
Boiler.—Diameter .... 60 in.
"   Thickness of Sheets .... $^5/_8$ & $^{11}/_{16}$ in.
"   Working Pressure 180
"   Fuel .... Soft Coal
Firebox.—Material .... Steel
"   Length .... 102 $^1/_8$ in
"   Width .... 42 in.
"   Depth .... F., 69½ in.; B., 58½ in.
"   Thickness of Sheets, sides .... $^3/_8$ in.
"   "   "   back .... $^3/_8$ in.
"   "   "   crown .... ½ in.
"   "   "   tube .... ½ in.
Tubes.—Number 280
"   Diameter .... 2 in.
"   Length .... 14 ft., 4½ in.
Driving Wheels.—Diameter Outside .... 56 in.
"   "   of Centre .... 50 in.
"   Journals .... 8½x11 in.
Engine Truck Wheels.—Diameter .... 30 in.
"   Journals .... 6x10 in.
Wheel Base.—Driving .... 13 ft.
"   Total Engine .... 24 ft. 9 in.
Weight.—On Drivers .... 116,850 lbs.
"   On Truck .... 33,930 lbs.
"   Total Engine 150,780
Tender.—Diameter of Wheels .... 33 in.
"   Journals .... 5x9 in.
"   Tank Capacity .... 4,000 gals.

CONSOLIDATION
FOR FREIGHT SERVICE.

Cylinders.—Diameter (high pressure) .... 15½ in.
"   "   (low pressure) .... 26 in.
"   Stroke .... 30 in.
"   Valve .... Balanced Piston
Boiler.—Diameter .... 68 in.
"   Thickness of Sheets .... $^{11}/_{16}$ & $^3/_4$ in.
"   Working Pressure 180
"   Fuel .... Soft Coal
Firebox.—Material .... Steel
"   Length .... 120 $^1/_8$ in
"   Width .... 42 in.
"   Depth .... F., 72¼ in.; B., 69¼ in.
"   Thickness of Sheets, sides .... $^3/_8$ in.
"   "   "   back .... $^3/_8$ in.
"   "   "   crown .... ½ in.
"   "   "   tube .... ½ in.
Tubes.—Number 321
"   Diameter .... 2 in.
"   Length .... 13 ft., 6 in.
Driving Wheels.—Diameter Outside .... 56 in.
"   "   of Centre .... 50 in.
"   Journals .... 8½x11 in.
Engine Truck Wheels.—Diameter .... 30 in.
"   Journals .... 6x10 in.
Wheel Base.—Driving .... 15 ft. 1 in.
"   Total Engine .... 23 ft. 9 in.
Weight.—On Drivers .... 164,585 lbs.
"   On Truck .... 19,325 lbs.
"   Total Engine 183,910
Tender.—Diameter of Wheels .... 33 in.
"   Journals .... 5x9 in.
"   Tank Capacity .... 4,500 gals.

The compound Ten-wheelers were "guaranteed to haul a load of 750 to 800 tons of cars and lading on a grade of 1% combined with curves of 4½ degrees, track and cars being in good condition."

The compound Consolidations were "guaranteed to haul a load of 1150 to 1200 tons, cars and lading, on a grade of 1 percent combined with curves of 4½ degrees, track and cars being in good condition."

These locomotives spent most of their working life on the trackage of the O.A. & P.S.

Passenger service between Madawaska and Depot Harbour was hauled by the Baldwin 4-4-0 locos. Many of the locomotives of the Canada Atlantic survived until the Grand Trunk Amalgamation with Canadian National. Most, however, had succumbed to the scrapper by the beginning of the Second World War.

Further information can be found on the Canada Atlantic Roster, which was compiled by the late W.G. Cole, a former engineer on the O.A. & P.S. Railway.

Unfortunately, no listing of freight or passenger equipment has currently come to light.

Canada Atlantic #607 was built by Taunton Locomotive Works in 1875. It had 62" drivers and weighed 110,000lbs. engine and tender. Algonquin Park Museum

Canada Atlantic #8. The only Mason Bogie on standard gauge in Canada. Eventually numbered 724 and Grand Trunk #1312, it was scrapped before 1913.

Canada Atlantic #652, formerly C.A.R. #10, one of the Rhode Island 2-6-0- type built January 1886. It had 57" drivers and total weight of 142,000lbs. Algonquin Park Museum #391

Canada Atlantic #9, another Rhode Island 2-6-0 built on the same order as #652. W.G. Cole Collection CRHA

A typical passenger train from the early years of the Canada Atlantic. Public Archives Canada #C 11597

Engine 15 with an early train on the O.A. & P.S. Public Archives Canada #PA 27298

One of the first locomotives purchased specifically for the O.A. & P.S. Baldwin built in 1898, this 4-6-0 had 56" drivers. Total weight was 229,000lbs. Harold K. Vollrath Collection

The 2-8-0 type purchased from Baldwin in 1898 and 1899 also had 56" drivers. Their total weight was 276,000lbs. Harold K. Vollrath Collection

This view shows ex-Canada Atlantic #619 after its rebuild in 1910. An Atlantic type #619 had 78" drivers, 56" trailing wheels and a total weight of 262,000lbs. Harold K. Vollrath Collection

*The Canada Atlantic had two 0-6-0 type switching engines. Numbered One and Two, they had 50"
drivers and weighed 125,000lbs. Harold K. Volrath Collection*

Although primarily used on the O.A. & P.S., the ten-wheelers sometimes strayed during the Grand Trunk years. Engine 1640, formerly O.A. & P.S. #629, is shown at Swanton, Vermont in 1914. This was still on ex-Canada Atlantic trackage. Harold K. Volrath Collection

Over the years all the locomotives received rebuilds. This view, taken at Belleville, Ontario in 1944, shows how ex-O.A. & P.S. #636 had changed. Harold K. Vollrath Collection)

A view of 2-8-0 Number 694 as she appeared in service. Public Archives Canada #C 29164

Grand Trunk Engine 1632, formerly O.A. & P.S. 698, hauling a work train loaded with rail in April 1920. Algonquin Park Museum #25

Grand Trunk 1323, formerly C.A.R. 611, was a typical passenger engine. Ontario Archives Acc. 10328, Tray 5 #38

Occasionally if more capacity was required, a 2-6-0 like Number 523 would be on the head end of the passenger train. Ontario Archives Acc. 10328, Tray 7 #38

ROAD NUMBERS			TYPE				WHEEL	WHEEL DIA. (in.)			
Orig.	Subs.	Final	Kind &	Class	BUILT	BUILDER	ARRGT	Drivers	Eng. Trucks	Tdr. Trucks	BOILER DIA. (in.)
1		1	S	A	8/87	Baldwin	0-6-0	50		33	48
2		2	S	A	2/89	Baldwin	0-6-0	50		33	52
3		3	S	B	7/98	Baldwin	0-4-0	51		33	54
4		4	S	B	7/98	Baldwin	0-4-0	51		33	54
5		5	S	B	7/98	Baldwin	0-4-0	51		33	54
6	606	10	P	P	/75	Baltimore & Ohio	4-4-0	61¼	26	33	45
1PS		607	P	P	1873/	Taunton	4-4-0	62	30	33	45
13		608	P	C	12/86	Baldwin	4-4-0	69	30	33	50
14		609	P	C	12/86	Baldwin	4-4-0	69	30	33	50
15		610	P	C	1/88	Baldwin	4-4-0	69	30	33	50
16		611	P	C	3/88	Baldwin	4-4-0	69	30	33	50
618		618	P	D	5/01	Baldwin	4-4-2	84¼	36&56	36	62
619		619	P	E	4/99	Baldwin	4-4-2	78	36&56	36	60
620		620	P	E	4/99	Baldwin	4-4-2	78	36&56	36	60
20		621	P	F	8/93	Baldwin	4-4-0	69	30	33	58
21		622	P	F	8/93	Baldwin	4-4-0	69	30	33	58
22		623	P	F	4/94	Baldwin	4-4-0	69	30	33	58
23		624	P	F	4/94	Baldwin	4-4-0	69	30	33	58
30	V&PL	625	P	F	4/95	Baldwin	4-4-0	69	30	33	58
25		626	P	F	10/96	Baldwin	4-4-0	69	30	33	58
26		627	P	F	10/96	Baldwin	4-4-0	69	30	33	58
1SL&A	24	628	P	G	2/96	Schenectady	4-4-0	67	30	33	58
629PS		629	F	H	4/98	Baldwin	4-6-0	56	30	33	60
630PS		630	F	H	4/98	Baldwin	4-6-0	56	30	33	60
631PS		631	F	H	4/98	Baldwin	4-6-0	56	30	33	60
632PS		632	F	H	4/98	Baldwin	4-6-0	56	30	33	60
633PS		633	F	H	4/98	Baldwin	4-6-0	56	30	33	60
634PS		634	F	H	4/98	Baldwin	4-6-0	56	30	33	60
635PS		635	F	H	4/98	Baldwin	4-6-0	56	30	33	60
636PS		636	F	H	4/98	Baldwin	4-6-0	56	30	33	60
637PS		637	F	H	4/98	Baldwin	4-6-0	56	30	33	60
638PS		638	F	H	4/98	Baldwin	4-6-0	56	30	33	60
9	80	651	F	I	1/86	Rhode Island	2-6-0	57	30	33	50
10	81	652	F	I	1/86	Rhode Island	2-6-0	57	30	33	50
11	82	653	F	I	1/86	Rhode Island	2-6-0	57	30	33	50
7	60	661	F	J	9/87	Rhode Island	2-6-0	54	30	33	52
8	62	662	F	J	9/87	Rhode Island	2-6-0	54	30	33	52
63PS		663	F	K	4/94	Baldwin	2-6-0	57	30	33	56
64PS		664	F	K	4/94	Baldwin	2-6-0	57	30	33	56
12	61	665	F	L	12/88	Baldwin	2-6-0	57	30	33	52
167	V&PL	667	F	K	6/95	Baldwin	2-6-0	57	30	33	56
168	V&PL	668	F	K	6/95	Baldwin	2-6-0	57	30	33	56
169	V&PL	669	F	K	6/95	Baldwin	2-6-0	57	30	33	56
70		670	F	K	10/96	Baldwin	2-6-0	57	30	33	56
71		671	F	K	10/96	Baldwin	2-6-0	57	30	33	56
31		681	F	M	7/89	Rhode Island	2-6-0	52½	30	33	54
32		682	F	M	7/89	Rhode Island	2-6-0	52½	30	33	54
33		683	F	M	7/89	Rhode Island	2-6-0	52½	30	33	54
690PS		690	F	N	6/98	Baldwin	2-8-0	56	30	33	68
691PS		691	F	N	6/98	Baldwin	2-8-0	56	30	33	68
692PS		692	F	N	6/98	Baldwin	2-8-0	56	30	33	68
693PS		693	F	N	6/98	Baldwin	2-8-0	56	30	33	68
694PS		694	F	N	6/98	Baldwin	2-8-0	56	30	33	68
695PS		695	F	N	6/98	Baldwin	2-8-0	56	30	33	68
696PS		696	F	N	7/99	Baldwin	2-8-0	56	30	33	68
697PS		697	F	N	7/99	Baldwin	2-8-0	56	30	33	68
698PS		698	F	N	7/99	Baldwin	2-8-0	56	30	33	68
699PS		699	F	N	7/99	Baldwin	2-8-0	56	30	33	68
700PS		700	F	N	8/99	Baldwin	2-8-0	56	30	33	68
701PS		701	F	N	8/99	Baldwin	2-8-0	56	30	33	68
702PS		702	F	N	8/99	Baldwin	2-8-0	56	30	33	68
703PS		703	F	N	8/99	Baldwin	2-8-0	56	30	33	68
100		710	F	O	9/93	Baldwin	2-6-0	57	30	33	64
8	4	724	S	P	7/77	Mason	06-6T	50		30	54

Assignments:
      PS: Parry Sound Colonization Railway
   V&PL: Vermont & Province Line Railroad
Acquisition:
  SL&A: St. Lawrence & Adirondack

CYLINDERS (in.)	WEIGHT (1000lbs.) On Drivers	Total Eng.	Eng. & Tdr.	SHOP NO.	SPECIF. NO.	ROAD NUMBERS C.A.R.	G.T.R. 1905	1910	G.T.R. Class	C.N.R.	C.N.R. CLASS	SCRAP DATE
17x24	72	72	117	8723	3823	*1	1316	2565	F5	Scrap		5/14
17x24	81	81	125	9810	6294	*2	1317	2566	F5	7084	O1a	7/25
16x24	80	80	140	16095	A95	3	1313	2555	F6	38	X7a	8/25
16x24	80	80	140	16096	A95	4	1314	2556	F6	39	X7a	8/25
16x24	80	80	140	16097	A95	5	1315	2557	F6	40	X7a Sold	2/24
16x22	47	70	110	-	-	*10	1318	Scrap	6/07			
16x24	47	70	110	596	-	*607	(1319)	Scrap	6/06			
17x24	50	76	132	8285	2885	608	1320	2119	J1	244	B9b	6/25
17x24	50	76	132	8287	2885	609	1321	2120	J1	245	B9b	6/25
17x24	50	80	141	9005	4740	*610	1322	2121	J1	246	B9b	12/24
17x24	50	80	141	9130	4740	*611	1323	2122	J1	247	B9b	11/24
13½x25x26	86	169	302	18977	A3113	618	1334	1502	B	Scrap		4/17
13&22x26	72	140	262	16678	A2538	*619	1332	1500	B1	Scrap		3/19
13&22x26	72	140	262	16679	A2538	*620	1333	1501	B1	Scrap		3/19
18x24	64	100	180	13700	7033	621	1324	2233	H2	304	B16a	7/25
18x24	64	100	180	13699	7033	*622	1325	2234	H2	305	B16a	6/25
18x24	64	100	180	13991	7033	*623	1326	2235	H2	306	B16a	7/25
18x24	64	100	180	13992	7033	624	1327	2236	H2	307	B16a	11/25
18x24	64	100	180	14296	7033	625	1328	2237	H2	308	B16a	7/25
18x24	68	106	176	15067	8702	626	1329	2238	H7	309	B16b	7/25
18x24	68	106	176	15068	8702	627	1330	2239	H7	310	B16b	11/25
18x24	69	109	209	4437	1593	628	1331	2240	H6	311	B17a	8/25
14&24x26	116	145	229	15912	9880	*629	1352	1640	A2	1168	G20a	10/41
14&24x26	116	145	229	15913	9880	*630	1353	1649	A2	1177	G20a	2/37
14&24x26	116	145	229	15914	9880	*631	1354	1641	A2	1169	G20a	1/36
14&24x26	116	145	229	15915	9880	*632	1355	1642	A2	1170	G20a	9/41
14&24x26	116	145	229	15916	9880	*633	1356	1643	A2	1171	G20a	10/41
14&24x26	116	145	229	15917	9880	*634	1357	1644	A2	1172	G20a	10/35
14&24x26	116	145	229	15918	9880	*635	1358	1645	A2	1173	G20a	12/35
14&24x26	116	145	229	15919	9880	*636	1359	1646	A2	1174	G20a	11/50
14&24x26	116	145	229	15920	9880	*637	1360	1647	A2	1175	G20a	12/35
14&24x26	116	145	229	15921	9880	*638	1361	1648	A2	1176	G20a	10/41
17x24	75	88	142	1609	590	651	1335	2342	E7	Scrap		7/22
17x24	75	88	142	1610	590	*652	1336	2343	E7	Scrap		6/19
17x24	75	88	142	1611	590	653	1337	2344	E7	497	D5a	6/25
18x24	82	94	154	1838	975	661	1338	2353	E5	Scrap 6/19		
18x24	82	94	154	1839	975	662	1339	2354	E5	Sold GTP 43,		3/14
18x24	84	100	174	13993	7405	663	1340	2356	E5	Sold GTP 44,		3/14
18x24	84	100	174	13994	7405	664	1341	2357	E5	495	D4a	7/25
18x24	74	88	144	8313	2889	665	1342	2355	E5	496	D4b	12/25
18x24	84	100	174	14310	8703	667	1343	2358	E5	Sold GTP 45,		3/14
18x24	84	100	174	14311	8703	668	1344	2359	E5	Sold GTP 46,		3/14
18x24	84	100	174	14313	8703	669	1345	2360	E5	Sold GTP 47,		3/14
18x24	88	106	176	15065	8703	670	1346	2361	E5	Sold GTP 48,		3/14
18x24	88	106	176	15066	8703	671	1347	2362	E5	Sold GTP 49,		3/14
19x24	85	102	167	2199	1496	*681	1348	2527	E2	499	D8a	12/25
19x24	85	102	167	2200	1496	*682	1349	2528	E2	500	D8a Sold 9/25 to Booth	
19x24	85	102	167	2201	1496	*683	1350	2529	E2	Sold		6/20
15½&26x30	164½	184	276	15955	9881	*690	1362	1625	D1	1957	M6a	11/35
15½&26x30	164½	184	276	15956	9881	*691	1363	1636	D1	1970	M6b	6/39
15½&26x30	164½	184	276	15957	9881	*692	1364	1626	D1	1958	M6a	12/35
15½&26x30	164½	184	276	15958	9881	*693	1365	1627	D1	1959	M6a	11/38
15½&26x30	164½	184	276	15959	9881	*694	1366	1628	D1	1964	M6b	8/39
15½&26x30	164½	184	276	15960	9881	*695	1367	1629	D1	1965	M6b	3/36
15½&26x30	164½	184	276	16937	9881	*696	1368	1630	D1	1966	M6b	11/35
15½&26x30	164½	184	276	16938	9881	*697	1369	1631	D1	1967	M6b	3/36
15½&26x30	164½	184	276	16939	9881	*698	1370	1632	D1	1960	M6a	12/35
15½&26x30	164½	184	276	16940	9881	*699	1371	1633	D1	1961	M6a	11/35
15½&26x30	164½	184	276	16954	9881	*700	1372	1637	D1	1962	M6a	2/36
15½&26x30	164½	184	276	16955	9881	*701	1373	1638	D1	1963	M6a	10/35
15½&26x30	164½	184	276	16956	9881	*702	1374	1634	D1	1968	M6b	10/35
15½&26x30	164½	184	276	16957	9881	*703	1375	1635	D1	1969	M6b	11/35
19x26	98	116	196	13689	7034	710	1351	2530	E1	501	D9a	6/27
16x22	100	100	156	586	-	*724	(1312)	Scrap	6/06			

*Locomotives known used on O.A. & P.S.

During the winter, some of the locomotives were equipped with snowplows. Public Archives Canada #PA 28054

For heavier snow removal, the Grand Trunk utilized Plow #98101.
Public Archives Canada #PA 42483

Other maintenance of way equipment included this portable railway steam shovel. Public Archives
Canada #C 27324

*The section crew at Canoe Lake riding on a converted pump car. The Casey Jones Railway Supply
Company offered single-cylinder gas engines to convert pump cars. These conversions often cost two or
three months of the section foreman's salary, as the railways did not consider them necessary.* Algonquin
Park Museum #38

The Ontario Fire Protection crew in Algonquin Park had its own speeder, equipped with fire fighting equipment. Algonquin Park Museum #1252

One of the few pictures of a Canada Atlantic van or caboose. W.G. Cole Collection CRHA

The O.A. & P.S. had no boxcars of its own. All the cars it required were leased from the parent company.
W.G. Cole Collection CRHA

It was quite common to see cars from other railways, particularly Central Vermont, on the Canada Atlantic system. The Vermont and Province Line Railroad, third car from the left, was the three-mile section of the Canada Atlantic which was inside the United States. Ontario Archives Acc. 10328, Tray 5 #39

There was no shortage of boxcars on the Canada Atlantic, and they all seem to have different paint schemes. Ontario Archives Acc. 10328, Tray 5 #20

The Canada Atlantic system included a steamship line. The S.S. Arthur Orr of the Canada Atlantic Transit Company is photographed at Depot Harbour around 1904. Public Archives Canada #PA 8561

CHAPTER 9
RUNNING EXTRA ON THE O.A.&P.S.

This chapter is written to provide a place for all the extra pieces of information that do not fit in the other chapters!

CHRONOLOGY OF IMPORTANT DATES

1882 — J.R. Booth organized Canada Atlantic Railway.

1888 — Completion of the C.A.R. and chartering of the Ottawa Arnprior and Renfrew and Ottawa and Parry Sound Railways.

1891 — Amalgamation of O.A. & R. Railway and O. & P.S. Railway into the Ottawa Arnprior and Parry Sound Railway.

1892 — J.R. Booth purchased Parry Sound Colonization Railway.

1895 — Completion of P.S.C. Railway.

1896 — Completion of O.A. & P.S. Railway to Scotia and takeover of the P.S.C. Railway.

1897 — January 7th: first through train, Ottawa to Rose Point on Parry Sound.

1898 — Completion of elevators and trackage to Depot Harbour.

1899 — O.A. & P.S. amalgamated with C.A.R., the parent company. The railway was now the largest privately owned railway in North America.

1899 — Organization of the Canada Atlantic Transit Company, a steamship line to transport grain and package goods to Depot Harbour.

1905 — Canada Atlantic system sold to the Grand Trunk Railway for fourteen million dollars, a loss of four million dollars to J.R. Booth. The C.A.R. still existed on paper for another eight years, while it was brought up to G.T.R. standards.

1906 — Capital expenditures for this year included:

New roundhouse, Madawaska $41,508.25
New roundhouse, Depot Harbour $38,879.75
New coal chutes, Madawaska $7,712.64
Depot Harbour elevator annex $78,769.58

1908 — Grand Trunk opened Highland Inn.

1913 — Camps Nominigan and Minnesing opened by G.T.R.

1913 — C.A.R. amalgamated with G.T.R.

1914 — Beginning of World War One. G.T.R. running troop trains through Algonquin. Guards were stationed on all bridges to prevent sabotage. Despite this, many derailments occurred.

1915 — Fifteen grain ships tied up for the winter at Depot Harbour. The ice was cut with saws to allow ships to be moved to the dock for unloading.

1916 — Derailment at Joe Lake put fifteen cars into the lake.

1917 — Deer were hunted and shipped out to supplement the Canadian meat supply.

1918 — Guards were removed from bridges at end of the war.

1923 — Grand Trunk Railway taken over by Canadian National Railways.

1923 — Minnesing Camp sold.

1931 — Nominigan Camp sold.

1931 — Ontario Department of Lands and Forests shipped one live beaver and one flatcar of evergreens to Toronto for the Canadian National Exhibition.

1933 — Cache-Two Rivers trestle condemned. Renewal cost of bridge would be $500,000.00. Through service discontinued.

1935 — Automobile with steel wheels operated during summer months only. One return trip a day was offered between Cache Lake (Algonquin Park Station) and Madawaska.

1936 — C.N.R. applied to the Board of Railway Commissioners for Canada for abandonment of trackage between Lake of Two Rivers and Ravensworth. Application was removed after a discussion by all parties concerned.

1940 — Track over Cache-Two Rivers trestle lifted.
1942 — Service discontinued between Two Rivers and Rock Lake.
1945 — Service discontinued between Rock Lake and Whitney.
1945 — Elevators and freight sheds at Depot Harbour burned.
1952 — Service discontinued between Scotia and James Bay Junction.
1952 — Canada Atlantic Transit Co., the steamship line, ceased to exist.
1955 — Trackage lifted Scotia to James Bay Junction and Whitney to Two Rivers.
1957 — Highland Inn dismantled.
1959 — Last train to Algonquin Park.
1959 — Rails lifted Kearney to Algonquin Park Station.
1959 — Steel Company of Canada started shipping Northern Ontario ore by train to Depot Harbour for transfer to ships.
Early
1960's — Caldwell Station dismantled accidentally when eastbound freight derailed just west of the station.
1963 — Last passenger service to Barry's Bay over O.A. & P.S. trackage.
1975 — Lifting of rail Kearney to Scotia Junction.
1979 — Last ore train to Depot Harbour.
1983 — Renfrew subdivision; Renfrew to Whitney, slated for abandonment.

Canadian National #3255. Ex-Canadian Government Railways 2-8-2. Pulling a special train of waney timber 1924. Algonquin Park Museum #1050

The completed elevators at Depot Harbour. The annex to the right of the central tower cost $78,769.58 in 1906. Ontario Archives Acc. 10328, Tray 5 #23

In 1931 the Ontario Department of Lands and Forests shipped one live beaver and a flatcar load of evergreens to Toronto for their display at the Canadian National Exhibition. Algonquin Park Museum #285 — #277

The Cache-Two Rivers trestle after track was lifted in 1940. Algonquin Park Museum #3593

CHAPTER 10
ANECDOTES ALONG THE RAILWAY

The following anecdotes were collected from people whose early years were affected by the railway. Some of these stories have been verified, others can only be verified by the memories of those who lived through them.

It has been mentioned in the Chronology that there were numerous derailments on the Grand Trunk Ottawa Division during the First World War. Although it has never been proven, the derailments were thought to be deliberate. It appears that the roadmaster in Ottawa, a German who was nicknamed the Crown Prince, ordered the section crews to remove the elevation from all the curves on the railway. As a result, the locomotives and equipment had a tendency to climb over the rails. This was his way of delaying troop trains and helping the Fatherland. During the investigations, the accidents were blamed on broken rails or improper handling of the equipment.

One such derailment in 1916 occurred at Joe Lake. A train consisting of fifteen empty cars followed by twenty loaded cars hopped the rails while crossing the embankment across the lake. The engine stayed on the ties, while the fifteen empties were pushed into the lake. The write-up stated a broken rail as the cause.

Although proper elevation was restored to the railway curves, the occasional derailment was inevitable. One such derailment was caused by cows lying in the tracks at night. A double-headed train hauling thirty-five flatcars came upon the cows unexpectedly. The engines derailed upon hitting one of the cows, and ended up in a mud pond with the first engine underneath the second. Five people — the first engineer, a brakeman, a fireman and two student firemen — were killed in this derailment. It is not known how many cows were killed.

Other accidents may have been caused by human error. Rule G prohibited drinking on the job; however, many of the railway workers at the turn of the century did enjoy strong drink in their off-duty hours. It is reported that the grain stolen from the Depot Harbour elevators often reappeared in the form of moonshine to be sold to the residents of the town. Moonshine was also common near Madawaska. One story tells of a baggageman who was purchasing moonshine from a local supplier who had boarded the train. The conductor came along as money was about to change hands, and asked if the baggageman had tested the drink for quality prior to making the deal. The baggageman admitted that he had not tasted it because of Rule G. The conductor proceeded to pour a portion of the brew onto the baggage-car floor, and lit it with a match. When the flame flared to over a foot high, he pronounced it was fit to drink.

Occasionally mechanical problems would develop with the equipment which could have caused terrible mishaps if circumstances had been different. In 1917 an eastbound freight train stopped at McCraney (Rainy Lake) for water. The engine was uncoupled and run up to the water tank. As the fireman was filling the tender, he felt the engine begin to move, so he shut off the water and dismounted from the engine. When the engine was clear of the water tank, the fireman noticed the engineer on the other side of the tracks. Each had thought the other was at the controls. The engine apparently had developed a leaky thottle and had taken off on its own. The train crew notified the dispatcher of the runaway and took off after it on a hand car.

The dispatcher was able to stop a westbound train at Canoe Lake. This train was to have met the eastbound freight at Brule Lake. The runaway meanwhile had climbed over the summit and raced through Brule Lake before running out of steam a short distance beyond. The engine crew regained control of the engine and returned to McCraney to pick up their train. This incident could have been much worse if the dispatcher had been unable to stop the westbound train at Canoe Lake.

The Bridge and Building Department of any railroad had a variety of problems to solve in order to maintain service. Work was always interrupted when their work trains were moved off the main line to allow scheduled trains to pass. This occurred up to eight times a day. Any work they did was not allowed to interfere with regular schedules. In 1907 the B. and B. Department constructed a new water tower and standpipe at Algonquin Park Station. By 1912 they realized that they were not receiving enough pressure at the standpipe to fill the larger engines and keep them on schedule. Their solution was to bring in large jacks and raise the half-full water tank and tower six feet higher. It was then placed on an extension made from timber. Water was left in the tank to enable them to fill passing trains with only the minor delay caused by attaching a temporary pipe extension.

The problem of this water tower could have been ignored if it had been left for a few years, because special instructions were issued restricting it to emergency use only. Algonquin Park Station was also the site of Highland Inn, and the following instructions were issued in the employees' timetable of 1922, to reduce noise in the area.

ALGONQUIN PARK BANJO SIGNALS

At Algonquin Park an automatic electric signal of the Banjo type (a signal that looked like a banjo), has been erected one mile east and one mile west of the stand pipe. These signals will go to stop as soon as passed by an engine or car moving toward Algonquin Park Station, and will remain at stop until rear car passes the stand pipe. A train approaching these signals, finding them at stop, will stop before passing them and then proceed expecting to find the main track occupied between the signal and the stand pipe.

We have also placed an electric bell 3500 feet east of the station, and another bell 2640 feet west of station. These bells can be rung by pushing a button in the telegraph office.

In order to discontinue engines whistling to call in flagmen, hereafter, when a train stops or is delayed on the main track under circumstances in which it may be overtaken by another train, the flagman must go back immediately to the point where bells are located and will at once place one torpedo (explosive warning device) on the rail, on the same side as the engineer of an approaching train, just beyond bell, and will remain in a position where he can hear the bell ring, until recalled, and when recalled he will place a second torpedo on the rail, not more than 200 feet from the first torpedo, and then return to his train. The flagman to be called in when his train is ready to start by a member of the crew (when directed by the engineer) pushing the button in the telegraph office instead of sounding the engine whistle.

At night or in stormy weather, or when conditions require it, the flagman will leave a fusee (flare) burning before returning to train.

Engine whistles must not be sounded in the vicinity of Algonquin Park Station unless to avoid accident or prevent injury to persons.

All trains must approach Algonquin Park expecting to find a train standing east or west of the stand pipe.

Freight trains will pull up within 100 feet if stand pipe before cutting engine off to take water.

SWITCHING, ALGONQUIN PARK

When hotel is open no switching must be done at Algonquin Park between the hours of 7.00 p.m. and 7.00 a.m. Trains having cars for this Station will ask Despatcher for instructions.

Freight trains must not take water at Algonquin Park unless in case of emergency. When passing by station, must have steam shut off and train moved with as little noise as possible.

It seems a lot of fuss to please a bunch of tourists. It would have been easier to build the inn elsewhere, away from any railway sidings in the first place.

It is stories and oddities like these that have made this a most interesting railway to research, and I hope, interesting to read about.

A view of Joe Lake derailment, which pushed cars into the lake like an accordion. Algonquin Park Museum #27

This view of Highland Inn shows its proximity to Algonquin Park Station and to the watering stand pipe. This explains why no whistles were blown in the vicinity of Algonquin Park Station. Algonquin Park Museum #752

MODELLER'S
APPENDIX A

The photographs and drawings in this section are included for the benefit of those who might wish to model something from the Ottawa Arnprior and Parry Sound Railway.

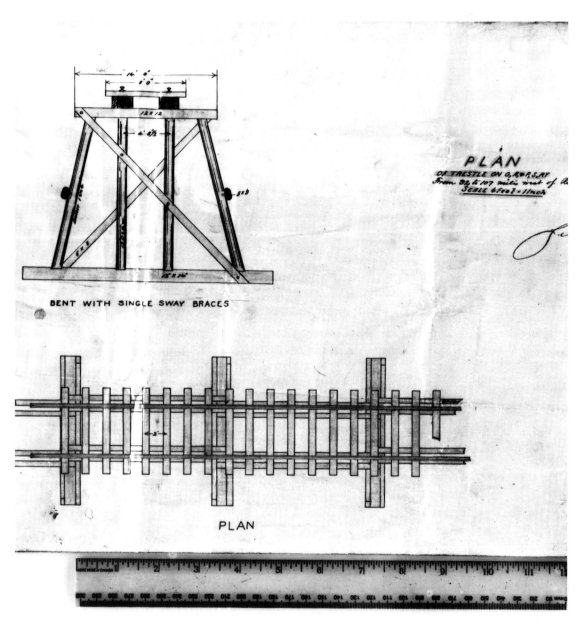

Plan of a typical O.A. & P.S. style trestle. National Map Collection 0016469

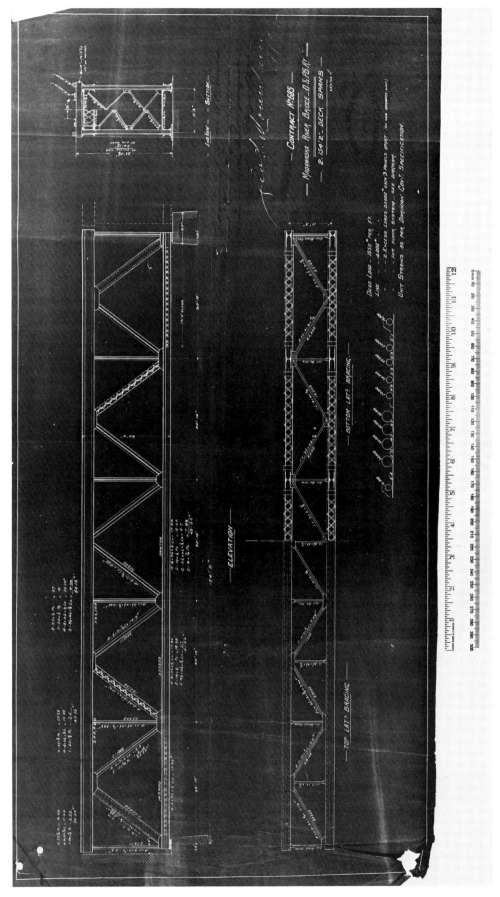

Plan of the Madawaska River Bridge. National Map Collection 0016472

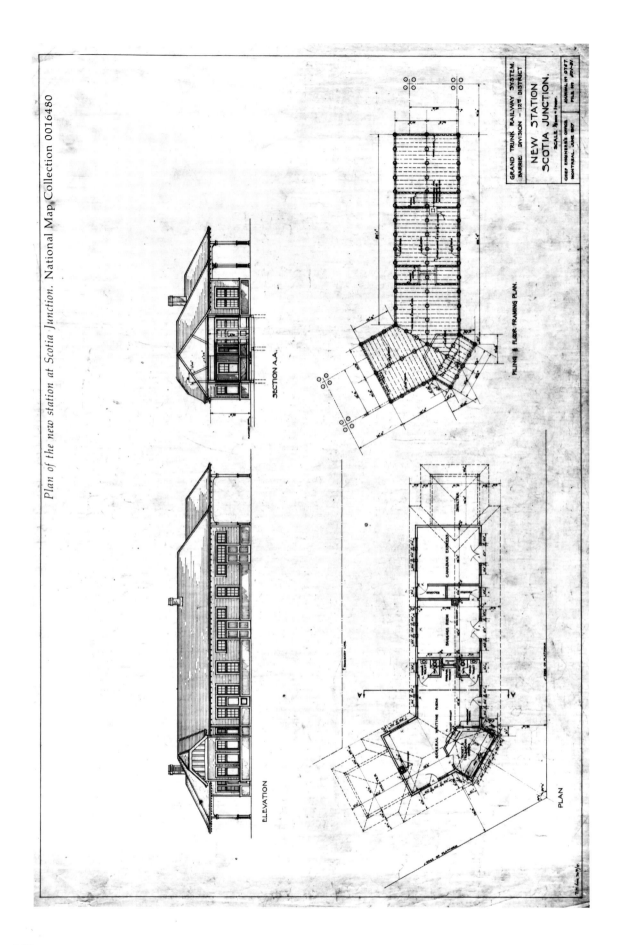

Plan of the new station at Scotia Junction. National Map Collection 0016480

The new station at Scotia Junction, built 1917. W.G. Cole Collection CRHA

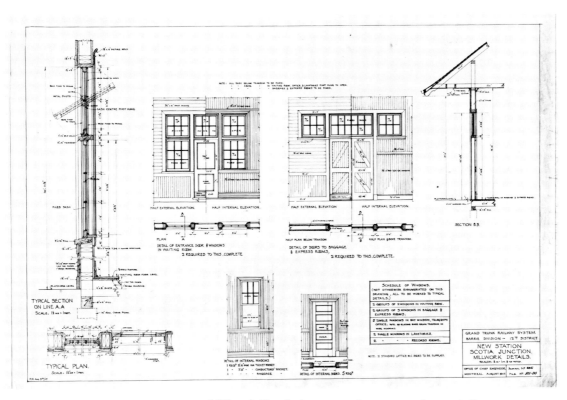

Millwork Details for new station. National Map Collection 0016481

Grand Trunk/Canadian National offices in Depot Harbour. Ontario Archives Acc. 10328, Tray 5 #43

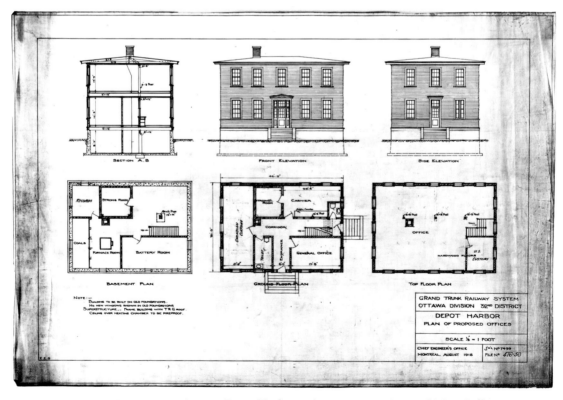

Plan of proposed offices Depot Harbour, August 1918. National Map Collection 0016470

A view of Algonquin Park Station. Algonquin Park Museum #507

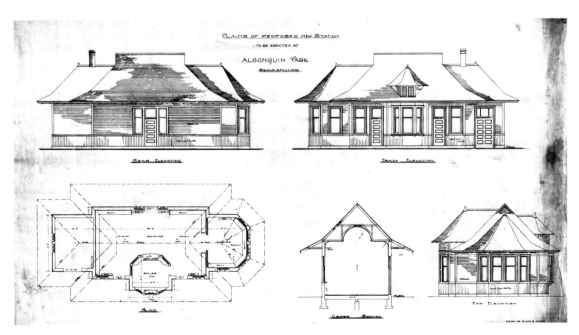

Plan of proposed new station for Algonquin, December 1907. National Map Collection 0016482

APPENDIX B

The Firemen and Enginemen who worked on the O.A. & P.S. during the Grand Trunk years.
Algonquin Park Museum #1080

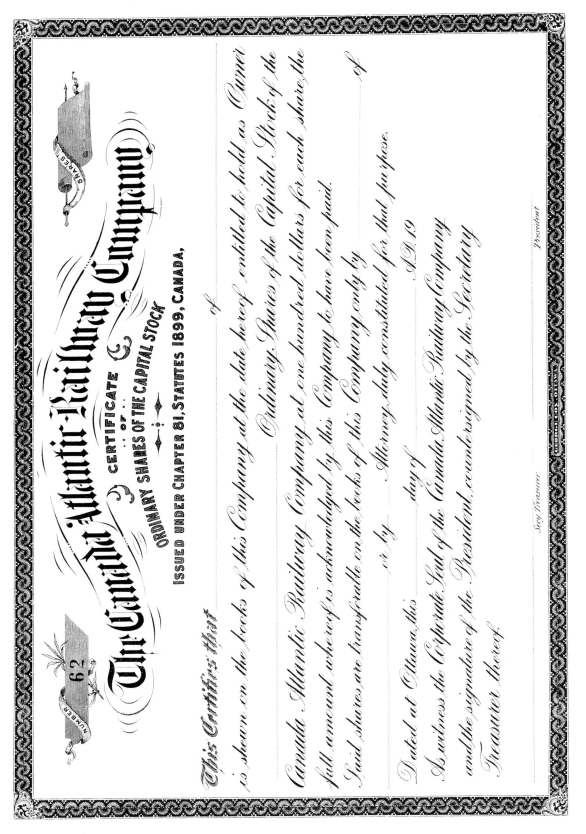

Blank share certificate for The Canada Atlantic Railway Company. Of the 65,000 common shares issued 60,417 belonged to J.R. Booth.

CANADA ATLANTIC
RAILWAY COMPANY

95	EMPLOYEES TIME TABLE	95

To take effect Sunday, June 18th, 1905, at 12.01 A.M.
EASTERN STANDARD TIME

STANDARD RULES

This Time Table is for the government and information of Employees only, and is not an advertisement of the time of any Train. The Company reserve the right to vary therefrom as circumstances may require. Read rules and special instructions carefully—important changes have been made. For General Rules and Regulations see Book of Rules.

Trains running East or South as indicated by Time Table heading will (unless otherwise specified) have the absolute right of track over trains of the same class running in the opposite direction. See Rules 384 and 385A.

E. J. CHAMBERLIN,	M. DONALDSON,	W. C. C. MEHAN,	F. L. LAMPLOUGH,
General Manager.	General Superintendent.	Train Master.	Chief Despatcher.

James Hope & Sons, Printers, Ottawa.

C.A.R. Employees Timetable #95, June 1905. Public Archives Canada RG 30 Deposit 34 Volume 2707-1 Item 14-A

MIDDLE DIVISION

Southbound Trains.   **Pembroke Branch.**   **Northbound Trains**

1st Class			Telegraph Offices. D Day N Night	Distance from Pembroke	Time Table No. 95 Effective June 18, 1905	Distance from Golden Lake	Telegraph Calls	1st Class		
47	45	43						44	46	48
Passeng'r	Passeng'r	Mixed.			STATIONS			Passeng'r	Passeng'r	Mixed.
Daily Ex. Sunday	Daily Ex. Sunday	Daily Ex. Sunday						Daily Ex. Sunday	Daily Ex. Sunday	Daily Ex. Sunday
P. M.	P. M.	A. M.			Leave Arrive			A. M.	P. M.	P. M.
5 10	1 45	7 35	D	.0	**PEMBROKE**	20.9	P R	11 25	3 05	8 25
f 5 21	f 1 56	f 7 50		6.3	6.3 Locksley	14.6		f 11 14	f 2 54	f 8 10
f 5 29	f 2 04	f 8 04		11.0	4.7 Wolto	9.9		f 11 06	f 2 46	f 7 56
5 45	2 20	8 25	D	20.9	9.9 **GOLDEN LAKE**	.0	A K	10 50	2 30	7 35
P. M	P. M.	A. M.			Arrive Leave			A. M.	P. M.	P. M.
Daily Ex. Sunday	Daily Ex. Sunday	Daily Ex. Sunday						Daily Ex. Sunday	Daily Ex. Sunday	Daily Ex. Sunday

Southbound Trains will have absolute right of track over trains of the same class running in the opposite direction
See Rules 384 and 385A. All trains will register at Pembroke and Golden Lake. Standard Clock at Pembroke.
Branch Trains when using Main Line at Golden Lake must protect against Main Line Trains.

Despatcher's Office, Ottawa. Telegraph Call, N. A.

3rd Class	2nd Class	1st Class	1st Class	Telegraph Offices D Day N Night	Distance from Depot Harbor	Time Table No. 95 Effective June 18, 1905 STATIONS	Distance from Ottawa	Telegraph Calls	1st Class	1st Class	2nd Class	3rd Class
65	67	57	53						52	56	68	66
Way Frt.	Mixed	Passeng'r	Passeng'r						Passeng'r	Passeng'r	Mixed	Way Frt.
Daily Ex. Sunday	Daily Ex. Sunday	Daily Ex. Sunday	Daily Ex. Sunday						Daily Ex. Sunday	Daily Ex. Sunday	Daily Ex. Sunday	Daily Ex. Sunday
A. M.	P. M.	A. M.	A. M.			Leave Arrive			P. M.	P. M.	P. M.	P. M.
8 10	3 00	8 00	7 30	D N	.0	DEPOT HARBOR	263.8	H R	9 00	7 10	12 40	5 20
f 8 28	s 3 15	s 8 08	f 7 38	D	3.5	3.5 Rose Point	260.3	R S	f 8 52	s 7 02	s 12 28	s 5 05
s 8 44	s 3 27	s 8 15	s 7 45		7.1	3.6 James Bay Junction	256.7		s 8 42	s 6 52	s 12 18	s 4 50
s 8 52	s 3 38	s 8 22	s 7 50	D N	9.6	2.5 Otter Lake	254.2	C Q	s 8 37	s 6 47	s 12 10	s 4 40
s 9 25	f 4 10	8 38	f 8 07		16.8	7.2 Beattys	247.0		f 8 22	6 32	f 11 46	4 10 / 4 00
s 9 34	f 4 16	s 8 43	s 8 12		18.7	1.9 Maple Lake	245.1		s 8 17	s 6 27	s 11 40	s 3 50
s 9 48	s 4 28	s 8 50	s 8 19	D N	21.8	3.1 Edgington	242.0	G U	s 8 10	s 6 20	s 11 29	s 3 38
s 10 16	s 4 52	s 9 04	s 8 33	D	28.2	6.4 Seguin Falls	235.6	S F	s 7 58	f 6 08	s 11 09	s 3 12
s 10 40 / 10 50	f 5 12	9 15	f 8 45		33.7	5.5 Bear Lake	230.1		f 7 46	f 5 58	f 10 50	s 2 50
s 11 07	f 5 25	9 23	f 8 53		37.2	3.5 White Hall	226.6		f 7 40	f 5 50	f 10 40	s 2 37
s 11 20	5 33 / 5 43	s 9 30	s 9 00	D N	40.2	3.0 Sprucedale	223.6	R U	s 7 32	s 5 43	s 10 30	s 2 24
11 43	6 03	9 43	9 11		45.8	5.6 Mud Lake	218.0		7 21	5 32	10 12	2 02
s 12 05 / 12 30	s 6 20	9 55	s 9 25 / 9 50	D N	51.2	5.4 Scotia Junction	212.6	N S	s 7 10 / 7 05	5 20	s 9 55 / 9 15 d	s 1 40 / 1 10
s 12 50 / 1 10	s 6 40 / 6 55		s 9 42	D	56.6	5.4 Kearney	207.2	K N	s 6 55		s 8 55	s 12 50
s 1 43	s 7 20		s 9 56	D	63.8	7.2 Ravensworth	200.0	R W	s 6 38		s 8 30	s 12 20
s 2 26	s 7 53		s 10 15	D N	73.6	9.8 Rainy Lake	190.2	R Y	s 6 18		s 7 58	s 11 42
s 3 02	s 8 20		s 10 31	D	81.7	8.1 Brule Lake	182.1	B U	s 6 03		s 7 28	s 11 09
s 3 28	f 8 40		f 10 45		87.8	6.1 Canoe Lake	176.0		f 5 50		f 7 08	10 45 / 10 35
s 4 05	s 9 10		s 11 00	D N	95.8	8.0 Algonquin Park	168.0	C H	s 5 34		s 6 40	s 10 02
s 4 55 / 5 10	s 9 50		s 11 24	D	107.7	11.9 Rock Lake	156.1	U F	s 5 10		s 6 01	s 9 13
s 5 40 / 6 00	s 10 24		s 11 46	D N	118.4	10.7 Whitney	145.4	W N	s 4 46		s 5 23	8 30 / 8 00
6 28	10 50		12 00		126.0	7.6 L'Amable Siding	137.8		4 30		4 58	7 30
f 6 45	f 11 08		f 12 09		130.5	4.5 Egan Estate	133.3		f 4 21		f 4 42	s 7 12
7 00	11 20		12 15	D N	133.6	3.1 MADAWASKA	130.2	M D	4 15		4 30	7 00
P. M.	P. M.	A. M.	P. M.			Arrive Leave			P. M.	P. M.	A. M.	A. M.
Daily Ex. Sunday	Daily Ex. Sunday	Daily Ex. Sunday	Daily Ex. Sunday						Daily Ex. Sunday	Daily Ex. Sunday	Daily Ex. Sunday	Daily Ex. Sunday

Eastbound Trains will have absolute right of track over trains of the same class running in the opposite direction.   See Rules 384 and 385 A.   All trains will register at Depot Harbor and Madawaska.   Standard Clocks at Depot Harbor and Madawaska.

Level Crossing with Grand Trunk Railway at Scotia Jct.   **First class trains will register at Scotia Jct.**

Draw Bridge at Rose Point.   During navigation, all trains must come to a full stop and get " All Right " signal before crossing.

D Nos. 53 and 57.   Despatcher's Office, Ottawa.   Telegraph Call, N. A.

No. 56 will obtain a clearance before leaving Scotia Jct

Eastbound Trains   MIDDLE DIVISION.   Westbound Trains

3rd Class	1st Class			Telegraph Offices D Day N Night	Distance from Madawaska	Time Table No. 95 Effective June 18, 1905 STATIONS	Distance from Ottawa	Telegraph Calls	1st Class			3rd Class
61	55	53	51						50	52	54	60
Way Frt.	Passeng'r	Passeng'r	Passeng'r						Passeng'r	Passeng'r	Passeng'r	Way Frt.
Daily Ex. Sunday	Daily Ex. Sunday	Daily Ex. Sunday	Daily Ex. Sunday						Daily Ex. Sunday	Daily Ex. Sunday	Daily Ex. Sunday	Daily Ex. Sunday
A. M.	P. M.	P. M.	A. M.			Leave Arrive			P. M.	P. M.	P. M.	P. M.
6 00	4 10	12 45	7 00	D N	.0	**MADAWASKA**	130.2	M D	¶ 12 30	¶ 4 00	9 10	7 40
6 45	4 35	1 12	7 25		12.4	12.4 Aylen Lake	117.8		12 04	3 34	8 44	7 00
s 7 20 / s 7 52	s 4 55	s 1 30	s 7 42	D N	21.6	9.2 Barrys Bay	108.6	B Y	s 11 43	s 3 12	s 8 25	s 6 25
s 8 20	s 5 09	s 1 44	s 7 55	D	28.1	6.5 Wilno	102.1	I N	s 11 28	s 2 59	s 8 12	s 6 00
s 8 55 / 9 10	s 5 28	s 2 02	s 8 12	D	36.4	8.3 Killaloe	93.8	W S	s 11 10	s 2 40	s 7 54	5 28 / 5 00
s 9 43	s 5 45	s 2 20	s 8 30	D	45.3	8.9 Golden Lake	84.9	A K	s 10 50	s 2 20	s 7 35	s 4 30 / 4 20
s 10 10 / 10 35	s 5 59	s 2 34	s 8 45	D N	53.2	7.9 Eganville	77.0	V I	s 10 35	s 2 05	s 7 21	s 3 50 / 3 30
s 11 03	f 6 12	f 2 47	f 8 58		60.5	7.3 Caldwell	69.7		f 10 23	f 1 54	s 7 08	f 3 04
s 11 14	s 6 18	s 2 52	s 9 03	D	63.5	3.0 Douglas	66.7	D O	s 10 18	s 1 49	s 7 03	s 2 52 / 2 40
f 11 37	f 6 29	f 3 03	f 9 13		69.2	5.7 Admaston	61.0		f 10 08	f 1 39	f 6 52	f 2 17
s 11 55	f 6 38	f 3 12	f 9 23	D N	74.3	5.1 Renfrew Jct.	55.9	J C	f 9 58	f 1 31	f 6 42	s 1 55
12 00 / s 12 30	s 6 40	s 3 15	s 9 25	D	75.4	1.1 **RENFREW**	54.8	R N	s 9 55	s 1 29	s 6 40	s 1 50 / 12 30
f 12 50	f 6 49	f 3 23	s 9 34		80.3	4.9 Goshen	49.9		f 9 46	f 1 20	f 6 31	f 12 09
s 1 04 / 1 14	s 6 57	s 3 30	s 9 40	D	84.1	3.8 Glasgow	46.1	G S	s 9 40	s 1 14	s 6 24	s 11 55
1 45 / s 2 10	s 7 11	s 3 44	s 9 53	D	91.8	7.7 **ARNPRIOR**	38.4	R	s 9 26	s 1 00	s 6 10	s 11 20 / 10 50
2 50 / s 3 20	s 7 20	s 3 53	s 10 02	D N	96.8	5.0 Galetta	33.4	G	s 9 17	s 12 52	s 6 02	s 10 30
3 45 / 4 15	s 7 28	s 4 03	s 10 10	D	101.4	4.6 Kinburn	28.8	K I	s 9 08	s 12 44	s 5 53	10 10 / 9 55
4 45 / s 5 00	s 7 43	s 4 18	s 10 25	D N	109.8	8.4 Carp	20.4	C	s 8 53	s 12 29	s 5 39	9 20 / s 8 40
5 19 / s 5 29	f 7 54	f 4 28	f 10 35		115.8	6.0 South March	14.4		f 8 42	f 12 19	s 5 29	s 8 18
f 5 40	f 8 01	f 4 35	f 10 42		120.9	5.1 Graham Bay	9.3		f 8 35	f 12 13	f 5 20	f 8 00
6 06	8 13	4 48	10 53	D N	127.4	6.5 Chaudiere Junction	2.8	O S	8 23	12 02	5 08	7 35
6 10	8 16	4 51	10 56	D N	128.5	1.1 **ELGIN STREET**	1.7	D S	8 20	11 59	5 05	7 30 / s 7 25
	8 20	4 55	11 00	D N	130.2	1.7 **OTTAWA**	.0	C D	8 15	11 55	5 00	7 20
P. M.	P. M.	P. M.	A. M.			Arrive Leave			A. M.	A. M.	P. M.	A. M.
Daily Ex. Sunday	Daily Ex. Sunday	Daily Ex. Sunday	Daily Ex. Sunday						Daily Ex. Sunday	Daily Ex. Sunday	Daily Ex. Sunday	Daily Ex. Sunday

Eastbound Trains will have absolute right of track over trains of the same class running in the opposite direction. See Rules 384 and 385A

All trains will register at Madawaska and Ottawa. No. 52 will stop on signal for passengers to points west of Madawaska.

All trains, except first class trains, will register at Elgin Street. Standard Clocks at Ottawa, Elgin Street and Madawaska.

Level Crossing with Kingston & Pembroke Railway at Renfrew Jct.

Level Crossing with Canadian Pacific Railway ¼ mile West of Arnprior (Interlocking Plant.) See Instructions, page 9.

Draw Bridge over Rideau Canal, at Elgin Street. During navigation, all trains must come to a full stop and get "All Right" signal before crossing.

Operation of Semaphores in Ottawa Yards are governed by General Superintendent's Circulars :—No. 449, dated March 28th, 1897. No. 632, dated September 2nd, 1898, and Supplementary to No. 632, dated March 22nd, 1899.

No. 60 will obtain a clearance before leaving Elgin Street. Operator at Elgin Street will register First Class Trains.

Despatcher's Office, Ottawa. Telegraph Call, N. A.

GRAND TRUNK RAILWAY SYSTEM
(Supt. O.D. 1)

BRIDGES, BUILDINGS, WATER STATIONS, FUEL STATIONS, Etc.

AND ALL

TRACK STRUCTURES

ON

OTTAWA DIVISION

J. H. JOHNSTON.
Master Bridges and Buildings.

M. S. BLAIKLOCK,
Engineer, Maintenance of Way

E. H. FITZHUGH,
Third Vice-President

M. DONALDSON,
Superintendent.

W. G. BROWNLEE,
Gen'l Trans. Manager.

CHAS. M. HAYS,
Second Vice-Pres. and Gen'l. Mgr.

138

Mileage from Alburgh Junction	Stations and Buildings	Description and Dimensions	When built	Remarks (Condition)
396.63	Depot Harbor.			
	Elevator..........	Galvanized iron, tar and gravel, concrete....... 80'x92'x149'..........	1896	1st class.
	Addition..........	80'x196' (under construction)..............	1896	
	Marine Tower......	Galvanized iron, tar and gravel, concrete....... 25'x16½'x139'........	1896	1st class.
	Gallery connecting Marine Tower and Elevator........	Galvanized iron, gravel... 79'x14'x10'..........	1895	1st class.
	Idler. Tower.......	Galvanized iron, tar and gravel, concrete........ 18½'x18½'x60'........	1896	1st class.
	Power House.......	Brick, tin, gravel........ 58'x110'x22'..........	1896	1st class.
	Smoke Stack.......	Sheet iron, concrete false, 129' high, 40½' diam. at base................	1896	1st class.
	Coal Bin..........	Frame.............. 320'x50'..............	1896	1st class.
	Coal Chutes.......	Fr., shgle, post.......... 69'x12½'......9 chutes.	1896	1st class.
	Coal Bin for Power House..........	Frame............... 22½'x22½'.............	1896	1st class.
	Store Room and Office..........	Fr., board, sill.......... 30½'x15½'x9'.........	1896	2nd class.
	Dwelling House.....	Fr., gravel, post......... 20½'x24½'x18'.........	1895	1st class.
	Kitchen (att'd).....	Fr., gravel, post......... 14'x28'x18'.......... 22 houses of above type.	1895	1st class.
	Closet.............	Fr., shgle, sill.......... 3'x5½'x8'........... 22 closets of above type.	1895	1st class.
	Dwelling House.....	Fr., gravel, post......... 26¾'x37'10"x18'.......	1895	1st class.
	Kitchen (att'd).....	Fr., gravel, post......... 26¾'x11'x9'......... 29 houses of above type.	1895	1st class.
	Closet.............	Fr., shgle, sill.......... 3'x5½'x8'........... 29 closets of above type.	189.	1st class.
	Dwelling House.....	Fr., shgle, post.......... 40¾'x20¾'x19'......	1895	1st class.
	Kitchen (att'd).....	Fr., shgle, post......... 10½'x14'x19'.........	1895	1st class.
	Outside Kitchen....	Fr., shgle, post......... 15⅝'x24'x11'.........	1895	1st class.
	Closet.............	Fr., shgle, sill.......... 3'x5½'x8'...........	1895	1st class.
	Dwelling House.....	Fr., shgle, post.......... 24¾'x20½'x18'.......	1895	1st class.
	Kitchen (att'd).....	Fr., shgle, post......... 27⅝'x14¾'x18'....... 19 of above type......	1895	1st class.
	Closet.............	Fr., shgle, sill.......... 3'x5½'x8'........... 19 of above type.....	....	1st class.
	Town Hall.........	Fr., gravel, stone......... 44'x38⅝'x34'........	1895	1st class.
	Shed (att'd).......	Fr., gravel, stone......... 9½'x9½'x9'.........	1895	1st class.
	Closet.............	Fr., shgle, post.......... 14½'x8½'x9'........ 2 of above type......	1895	1st class.
	Pump House.......	Brick, gravel, concrete.... 21½'x10½'x13'........	1895	1st class.
	Bunk House.......	Fr., gravel, stone........ 30½'x99'x34'.........	1895	1st class.
	Addition..........	Fr., gravel, stone........ 30½'x23'x34'.........	1895	1st class.
	Closet.............	Fr., shgle, post.......... 14½'x8½'x9'........	1895	1st class.
	Butcher Shop......	Fr., gravel, post......... 16¾'x30¾'x12'........	1895	1st class.
	Post Office........	Fr., gravel, stone......... 24½'x16½'x12'........	1895	1st class.
	General Store......	Fr., gravel, stone........ 30½'x50½'x22'........	1895	1st class.
	Out House, (att'd)..	Fr., gravel, stone........ 9½'x9½'x8½'........	1895	1st class.
	Roadmaster's Office and Barber Shop..	Fr., shgle, post.......... 36½'x20½'x22'......	1895	1st class.
	Dwelling House.....	Fr., shgle, post.......... 20½'x24½'x18'........	1895	1st class.

Mileage from Alburgh Junction	Stations and Buildings	Description and Dimensions	When Built	Remarks (Condition)
	Kitchen (att'd)	Fr., shgle. post 24'x12½'x8'. 10 of above type	1895	1st class.
	Closet	Fr., shgle. post 3'x5½'x8'. 10 of above type	1895	1st class.
	Hose House	Fr., shgle, sill 7¼'x9'x8'	1895	1st class.
	Station	Fr., tin, post 26¼'x19½'x9', 1 story	1895	1st class.
	Freight Shed (att'd)	Fr., tin, post 19½'x49½'x9'	1895	1st class.
	Coal Shed	Fr., tin, post 13½'x8½'x7'	1895	1st class.
	Platform	3,100 sq. ft.	1895	
	Coal Chute	Frame, 16½'x16'	1895	
	Switchman's House	Fr., shgle, post 16½'x18¾'x9'	1895	1st class.
	Closet	Fr., shgle, sill 6'x4½'x7'	1895	1st class.
	Car Repair Shop	Two old box cars	1895	
	Sand Building	Fr., shgle, sill 14½'x16'x13'	1895	1st class.
	Hose Tower	Fr., gravel, post 14¾'x14¾' at base, 42' ht.	1895	1st class.
	Stable	Fr., shgle, post 26½'x37'x21'	1895	1st class.
	Shoe Store	Fr., shgle, sill 18½'x14½'x10'	1895	1st class.
	Oil House	Tin, shgle, post 20¼'x40½'x11'	1895	1st class.
	Office (att'd)	Fr., shgle, sill 9¼'x12½'x11'	1895	1st class.
	Dwelling House	Fr., shgle, post 24½'x24½'x16'	1895	3rd class.
	Freight Office	Fr., gravel, post 31⅜'x45'x34'	1895	1st class.
	Freight Shed No. 1	Fr., gravel, post 600'x80'x16'	1895	2nd class.
	Freight Shed No. 2	Fr., gravel, post 700'x80'x16'	1895	2nd class.
	Platform at Freight Sheds	7,800 sq. ft.	1895	
	Boarding House	Fr., gravel, stone 45½'x74¾'x34'	1895	1st class.
	Dining Room (at'd)	Fr., gravel, stone 75½'x54'x34'	1895	1st class.
	Kitchen (att'd)	Fr., gravel, stone 57'x43'x15'	1895	1st class.
	Engine House for Laundry (att'd)	Fr., gravel, stone 36'x16'x13'	1895	1st class.
	Covered Way connecting Kitchen & Hotel	Fr., gravel, stone 9½'x13½'x12'	1895	1st class.
	Dwelling House	Fr., shgle, post 25½'x14'x12'	1895	3rd class.
	Dwelling House	Fr., shgle, stone 24½'x16½'x18'	1895	1st class.
	Kitchen (att'd)	Fr., shgle, stone 20½'x16½'x18'	1895	1st class.
	Outside Kitchen (att'd).	Fr., shgle, post 14½'x20½'x10'	1895	1st class.

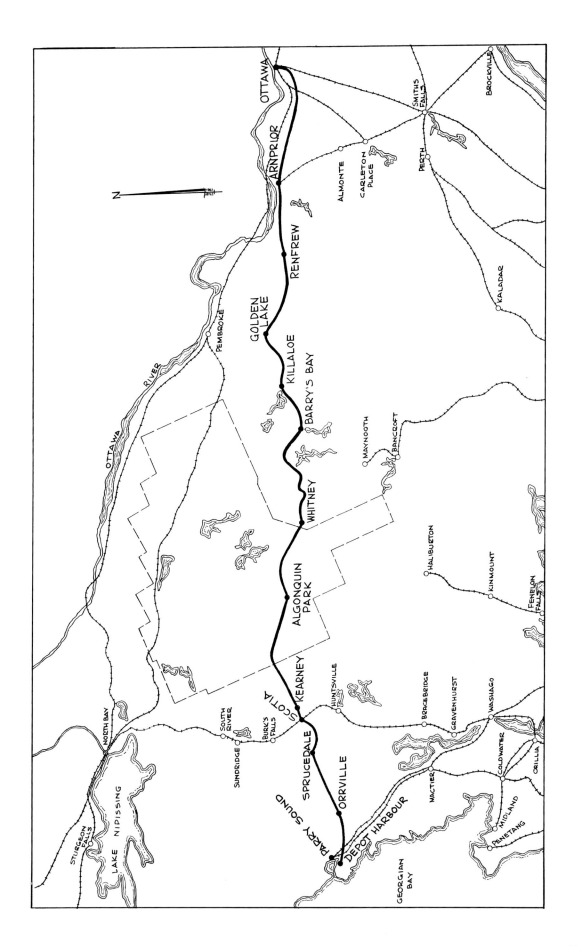

N

OTTAWA
ARNPRIOR
RENFREW
GOLDEN LAKE
KILLALOE
BARRY'S BAY
WHITNEY
ALGONQUIN PARK
KEARNEY
SCOTIA
SPRUCEDALE
ORRVILLE
PARRY SOUND
DEPOT HARBOUR

SMITHS FALLS
BROCKVILLE
CARLETON PLACE
ALMONTE
PERTH
KALADAR
MAYNOOTH
BANCROFT
HALIBURTON
KINMOUNT
FENELON FALLS
HUNTSVILLE
BRACEBRIDGE
GRAVENHURST
WASHAGO
COLDWATER
ORILLIA
MACTIER
MIDLAND
PENETANG

PEMBROKE
OTTAWA RIVER
NORTH BAY
SOUTH RIVER
BURK'S FALLS
SUNDRIDGE
STURGEON FALLS
LAKE NIPISSING
GEORGIAN BAY

141

ACKNOWLEDGEMENTS

I wish to acknowledge the cooperation, assistance and encouragement that I have received from my family and friends. In particular I wish to thank:

My parents, Dr. Iain M. MacKay and M. Jeanne MacKay
My aunt, Elizabeth Y. MacKay
My brother, Roderick I. MacKay
My good friend, Herb Jackman
and most of all
My wife, Patricia

REFERENCES

The Ottawa Morning Journal, Wednesday, December 9, 1925

Public Archives Canada, Record Group 12 Volumes 1879, 1880
          File 3268-70

Public Archives Canada, R.G. 30, Volume 217, 218

Public Archives Canada, Record Group 46 Volumes 998, 1169, 1222, 1291

Algonquin Park Chronology by Roderick MacKay, published in Summer 1980 issue Ministry of Natural Resources publication YOUR FORESTS.

Personal Conversations with:
          Mr. T. Elliot — Sprucedale
          Mr. Jack Wilson — Bear Lake
          Mr. Robert Palen — Parry Sound
          Mr. Tom Graves — Parry Sound
          Mr. Poole — Parry Sound
          Mr. Dave Thomas — Parry Sound

Tape Recorded Interview with:
          Mr. Ernie Montgomery — Madawaska